Psychology's Feminist Voices from Turkey

Ayçe Feride Yılmaz (ed.)

Psychology's Feminist Voices from Turkey
Knowledge, Activism, and Transformative Practices

Verlag Barbara Budrich
Opladen • Berlin • Toronto 2025

All rights reserved. No part of this publication may be reproduced, stored in or introduced into a retrieval system, or transmitted, in any form, or by any means (electronic, mechanical, photocopying, recording or otherwise) without the prior written permission of Verlag Barbara Budrich. Any person who does any unauthorized act in relation to this publication may be liable to criminal prosecution and civil claims for damages.

You must not circulate this book in any other binding or cover and you must impose this same condition on any acquirer.

A CIP catalogue record for this book is available from
Die Deutsche Nationalbibliothek (The German National Library):
https://portal.dnb.de.

Carbon compensated production

© 2025 by Verlag Barbara Budrich GmbH, Opladen, Berlin & Toronto

       ISBN 978 – 3 – 8474 – 3158 – 9 (Paperback)
       eISBN 978 – 3 – 8474 – 3309 – 5 (PDF)
       DOI   10.3224/84743158

Verlag Barbara Budrich GmbH
Stauffenbergstr. 7. D-51379 Leverkusen Opladen, Germany | info@budrich.de | www.budrich.de

86 Delma Drive. Toronto, ON M8W 4P6 Canada | info@budrich.de | www.budrich.eu

Cover design and cover image by Bettina Lehfeldt, Kleinmachnow –
    www.lehfeldtgraphic.de
Typesetting by Anja Borkam, Langenhagen – kontakt@lektorat-borkam.de
Printed in Europe on FSC®-certified paper by Libri Plureos, Hamburg

Table of Contents

Preface 7

Büşra Yalçınöz-Uçan
Finding Feminism in Research and Psychotherapy:
Reflections on Violence, Trauma, Vulnerability, and Healing 13

Leyla Soydinç
Feminist Psychotherapies in Addressing Violence against Women 27

Şahika Yüksel
A Feminist Voice in Mental Health from Turkey:
Complicating Mainstream Knowledge and Practice 47

Ayşe Dayı
From Feminist Clinics to Women's Healing Circles:
Women's Reproductive and Holistic Health from 70s to Today 61

Ayçe Feride Yılmaz
Solidarity on a Thorny Road: Becoming a Feminist Psychologist
in Turkey 75

Özden Melis Uluğ
Doing Research on Feminism, Activism and Social Change
for Gender Equality: Reflections of a Researcher from Turkey 109

Doğa Eroğlu-Şah
Navigating The Developmental Maze: A Feminist Journey
through Challenges 127

Authors 145

Index 149

Preface

In tandem with the scant first-wave women's movement, the burgeoning secular Republic of Turkey abolished Sharia law and recognized women's civil and political rights by 1934. This enabled a limited number of elite women to be recruited into sex-typed professions, overshadowing men of lower social sectors and bolstering the nation's modern ideology (Boratav, 2011; Çakır 2021). Nevertheless, reluctant to fully eliminate structural barriers against public participation, the modernizing state simultaneously ignored the overwhelming majority of women's subordination in society, culture and the private sphere through traditional gender norms, social segregation and the surveillance of female sexuality. The decades of rapid social change marked by urbanization and industrialization have not been accompanied by a similar rate of transformation of cultural values, norms and attitudes in terms of traditional interpersonal, gender and family relations (Sunar & Fisek, 2005). Therefore, the enduring historical characteristic of Turkish society as a patriarchal culture persisted, placing significant expectations on women to uphold traditional roles within marriage, family, and motherhood. In Turkey, women continue to face grave challenges stemming from cultural norms, cultural and religious conservatism, and patriarchal structures such as underage and forced marriages, barriers to education, sexual harassment, domestic and honor-based violence.

The feminist movement in Turkey has significantly consolidated itself over the years and achieved pivotal legislative gains in terms of empowering women. Feminism has also strongly permeated the macro social sciences such as sociology, political science, international relations and economics. Nevertheless, psychology, psychoanalysis, and psychiatry, as fields with the potential to forefront and politicize women's experiences and mental health issues within the broader sociopolitical context, have largely maintained their mainstream and apolitical stances, and much work in these realms remains as individual initiative. A minority of clinical psychologists, psychiatrists, and psychoanalytically oriented professionals perform their work based on feminist perspectives in their private practice, women's shelters, different NGOs, and engage in activism and advocacy research primarily focused on various forms of violence against women. As is the case with clinical psychology, vis-a-vis the stringent gatekeeping for research mirroring U.S. mainstream psychology, only a limited number of social psychology scholars investigate issues such as sexism and violence against women from a feminist perspective. There is a restricted quantity of gender courses available within psychology departments, as well as a scarcity of theses and published works pertaining to gender issues (Boratav, 2011).

This compilation is based on the symposium titled "Psychology's Feminist Voices from Turkey: Complicating Mainstream Knowledge and Practice," which took place on the 11th and 12th of January, 2024 at the Kilian-Köhler Center at Ruhr University Bochum. It comprises works from a sample of the small constituency of feminist scholars and activists who have been able to problematize and transcend mainstream approaches in clinical, social, developmental psychology, psychiatry, and psychoanalysis. The authors include individuals who attempted to critically negotiate with positivism in mainstream psychology, the orthodoxy in classical psychoanalysis and the biomedical framework in psychiatry, challenging hierarchical institutional relationships and expanding their fields by incorporating feminist understandings in their work. The profiles also feature individuals who incorporated their research into their feminist activism against gender-based discrimination and violence.

The efforts of contributors question intra-individual, intrapsychic, and biomedical theories and applications within a contextualized framework that aims to transform clinical practice into a space for healing, empowerment, solidarity, and resistance. They linked their clinical practice with rigorous and socially equitable research in order to support wider feminist politics in the public domain and civil society, acknowledging the interconnected nature of these endeavors. Their efforts are all the more crucial in Turkey's contemporary deteriorating landscape of increased gender-based violence and femicides, exacerbated by the government's anti-gender politics. This political situation reached its climax with the arbitrary decision to withdraw from the Council of Europe's Istanbul Convention on Preventing and Combating Violence against Women and Domestic Violence in 2021, and is evident in the current discussions regarding the potential annulment of Law 6284 on Protection of Family and Prevention of Violence against Women. On top of these, the implementation of the present protective and prosecutory legislation remains consistently ineffective as local law enforcement agencies neglect or ignore legal procedures and measures when it comes to gender-based violence. Thus, the authors' dedicated, extensive, and enduring feminist efforts, along with their incorporation of feminist psychology knowledge in both research and practice, combined with feminist political advocacy for women's rights, dignity, and empowerment, serve to fill a crucial gap in Turkey's challenging environment for women's rights.

The book starts with a piece by a clinical psychologist and researcher, Dr. Büşra Yalçınöz Uçan, who traces her evolving relationship with feminism through personal experiences, academic work, and therapeutic practice. Drawing on feminist theories and intersectionality, she highlights her research on decisions to stay or leave in cases of intimate partner violence, enabling an understanding of gender-based violence not from individual-level trauma perspectives, but as a product of broader structural inequalities. She also delves into the intersection of feminism and psychoanalysis from the perspective of a psychoanalytically oriented psychotherapist, reflecting on the challenges and possibilities of integrating these two fields. She sheds light on the role of psychoanalysis and feminism in the recognition of both personal and sociopolitical traumas, and in promoting a creative space. In that space, she emphasizes the importance of bearing and acknowledging both internal and external realities, a space where empathy and understanding coexist with the recognition of broader societal injustices. Ultimately, she underscores that despite the contradictions between psychoanalysis and feminism, both offer pathways for understanding and transformation, and provide opportunities for agency, hope, and resistance in the face of an often- unaccommodating external reality.

Leyla Soydinç traces the trajectory of the development of feminist therapies, where the initial manifestation of gender-based trauma in hysteria studies was critically reappropriated by the feminist movement and its consciousness-raising groups, along with psychoanalytic feminism. She discusses the impacts of male violence on women's mental health, underscoring that women's mental health challenges should not be explored through essentialist frameworks, but rather through examining systemic discrimination, power imbalances, and social control inherent in patriarchal configurations. She explains how an egalitarian and empowering relationship in feminist psychotherapy connects social transformation to individual empowerment through investigations of male violence, power imbalances, and gender roles. She points out how these principles are embodied in Mor Çatı Women's Shelter Foundation (Purple Roof), one of Turkey's leading feminist organizations dedicated to combating male violence and standing in solidarity with women who are survivors of violence through the implementation of feminist politics. As a feminist therapist and activist, she highlights how Mor Çatı's psychological support contributes to the broader feminist political movement by challenging societal norms related to violence.

Professor Dr. Şahika Yüksel describes the process by which her conventional approach to mental health, influenced by her training in traditional psychiatry, evolved following her involvement in the feminist movement and exposure to feminist literature. She details her endeavors to incorporate feminist viewpoints into the mental health field in Turkey, working in partnership with prominent mental health organizations to reform these establishments and promote societal transformation concerning gender-based violence and discrimination. Consequently, she outlines the ways in which feminist mental health professionals advocate for legal and institutional reform through a comprehensive approach, which includes organizing social support programs, conducting public education campaigns, collaborating with NGOs, and promoting progressive educational strategies for mental health practitioners. As a feminist psychiatrist and activist with decades of experience, she explores various measures at individual, community, and global levels to support survivors of gender-based violence. She emphasizes key principles such as the selection of culturally appropriate and cost-effective therapeutic interventions, the acknowledgment of violence as a violation of human rights, and the promotion of economic and educational empowerment.

Dr. Ayşe Dayı traces the evolution of women's reproductive healthcare from the 1970s Women's Health Movement to feminist clinics, emphasizing empowerment, dignity, and criticizing medicalized practices. Based on research from feminist health centers in the U.S., she highlights how empowerment in reproductive care is experienced through safety, emotional support, and holistic care. Her contribution further examines the impact of neoliberal health reforms and conservative politics on women's reproductive rights and access to dignified healthcare, drawing connections between the U.S. and Turkey. Drawing on her researcher and activist identities, she advocates for a holistic, non-patriarchal approach to reproductive care, where women receive support in a nurturing environment that integrates mind, body, and spirit. She recounts how she enacts this goal by facilitating women's healing circles in Berlin, aimed at reconnecting women with their authentic power and exploring themes like gender, sexuality, menstruation, and childbirth. These circles, combining meditation, movement, art, and shared experiences, focus on healing cultural wounds caused by patriarchal systems and empowering women through collective exploration and self-expression.

In my contribution, I report the results of a qualitative study conducted with four feminist psychologists who work or volunteer at the Mor Çatı Women's Shelter Foundation. The study explores the ways in which they have incorporated their professional identities with their feminist beliefs and activism, as well as how they have critiqued or moved beyond their mainstream education and training. The research indicates the significant shortcomings and limitations of traditional psychological and psychoanalytic approaches, and highlights the essential role of feminist clinical perspectives in addressing the widespread issue of gender-based violence and oppression in Turkey. As feminist psychology has considerably developed and expanded in Western contexts, showcasing the endeavors and obstacles encountered by feminist psychologists in a non-Western context also underscores the significance of international feminist psychology and transnational solidarity.

Dr. Ozden Melis Uluğ presents a compelling case for the use of research as a feminist instrument in addressing gender disparities, advocating for feminism, and challenging discriminatory practices. In presenting her various research endeavors on how collective action for gender equality takes place and how solidarity in collective action between different disadvantaged groups occurs in authoritarian contexts like Turkey, she also discusses how her own collective action experiences have shaped her researcher and activist identities, as well as how her intersecting feminist, activist, and researcher identities combine and inform each other. Utilizing the examples from her research, she outlines various obstacles in the examination of collective action in complex environments such as Turkey, presenting conceptual, methodological, and contextual challenges while suggesting potential directions for future research in feminist collective action studies.

The book ends with a piece on methodological critique and a case for turning research into a feminist act. Dr. Doga Eroglu Sah delves into a profound contemplation of the process of her doctoral thesis. She emphasizes the dynamic, interactive, intersubjective, and transformative processes that form the basis of the research experience, which are often overlooked in the final output of psychological studies due to the strong influence of the positivist paradigm. Accordingly, she discusses the challenges of integrating a social constructivist perspective into her project while negotiating with the dominant positivism imposed by academic institutions and departmental relations characterized by hierarchical and ideological structures. Providing a compelling methodological critique, she thereby politicizes the imposition of positivism by psychology departments, a worldwide phenomenon, and challenges the normalization of the fact that students interested in exploring alternative and critical perspectives in psychology, such as feminist psychology and masculinity studies, as well as alternative epistemologies like social constructivism, are constrained by the expectations of a strict positivist paradigm. Meanwhile, from a feminist perspective, she offers a thoughtful account of reflexivity regarding the interviewing encounter and how research can contribute to feminist goals.

In conclusion, the contributions presented in this compilation highlight the critical role of feminist perspectives in reshaping psychological, psychiatric, and psychoanalytic and academic practices. Despite the challenges posed by Turkey's patriarchal culture and restrictive institutional frameworks, the authors exemplify how feminist scholars and activists have navigated and challenged these structures, using their work to advocate for women's rights and address gender-based violence. Through a combination of research, practice, and activism, they have not only advanced feminist psychology but also contributed to broader social change. Their efforts are particularly vital in the current political climate, where gender-based violence and femicides are escalating, underscoring the urgency of their feminism in both mental health and society at large. The book demonstrates the potential of feminist knowledge to disrupt and transform mainstream psychological approaches and offers a powerful model for integrating activism with scholarly work to promote social change and gender justice.

References

Boratav, H. B. (2011). Searching for feminism in psychology in Turkey. In A. Rutherford, R. Capdevila, V. Undurti, & I. Palmary, (Eds.), *Handbook of international feminisms: Perspectives on psychology, women, culture, and rights* (pp. 17-36). Springer New York

Çakır, S. (2021). *Osmanlı Kadın Hareketi*. İstanbul, Metis Yayınları.

Sunar, D., & Fisek, G. (2005). Contemporary Turkish families. In U. Gielen &J. Roopnarine (Eds.), *Families in global perspective* (pp. 169-183). Allyn & Bacon/Pearson.

Finding Feminism in Research and Psychotherapy: Reflections on Violence, Trauma, Vulnerability, and Healing

Büşra Yalçınöz-Uçan

GBV-MIG Canada Research Program, Saint Mary's University, Halifax Regional Municipality, Nova Scotia, Canada

> [Feminism] "as happening in the very places that have historically been bracketed as not political... every room of the house can become a feminist room, in who does what where... feminism is wherever feminism needs to be... where did we find feminism, or where did feminism find us?" (Ahmed, 2017, p. 3-4).

This chapter unfolds my journey as a clinical psychologist and researcher—a path where I sought and found feminism and where I was found by feminism. It is a story of struggle, a constant one, both internal and external, of shaping myself as a feminist. It is a story of becoming—not without ambivalence, tensions, doubts, uncertainties, confusion, and anger. It is also a story of relationships, connections, and guidance—of being heard, understood, and supported. These stories reflect how I sometimes lose my grip on feminism, how I find my way back to it—or have it find me—and how I continue to learn to own and use it more skillfully.

In this chapter, I explore how I relate to feminism—first through my research on trauma, violence, and well-being, and then in therapeutic spaces, where I listen to my clients as a psychoanalytically oriented psychotherapist. However, before these, I will start with the story of why I need feminism and what it means to me.

From Personal to the Political: Lived Experiences and Definitions

The labor required to write this chapter was not solely academic or intellectual—perhaps it never is. Feminist writing, or feminist work more broadly, always entails an autoethnographic and emotional aspect (Davids & Willemse, 2014). The same can be said for psychoanalytic writing and practice. Whatever the task, engaging with it becomes an embodied, self-reflective practice (Rice, 2009). Thus, writing this chapter, at the intersection of my feminism and psychoanalytic thinking, like much of the work I do, is deeply personal, embedded within the specific particularities of my life, and involves a revisiting of personal stories—stories of harm, vulnerability, trauma, but also of learning, connecting, and healing.

My involvement with feminism began when I was an undergraduate psychology student in Turkey. I cannot pinpoint exactly how it started—I don't recall my first feminist readings or the time I began identifying as a 'feminist.' However, I do remember certain moments, moments when feminism drew near to me, without me fully realizing it at that time. One such moment was during an undergraduate family psychology course, where the professor opened up the lecture with a series of questions: "What is a family? Is a heterosexual couple not having a child a family? Is a man living on the street with his dog a family? What about a single mother and her daughter? Two men living together, are they a family?" I grew up in a traditional, working-class household with practicing Muslim parents. One thing my father always said about the meaning of life was that it lies in having a family—a family including a man, a woman, and children (and plurality here is crucial). Coming from this background, I recollect how I encountered these questions with a sense of provocation and excitement. Ahmed (2017) defines feminism as "sensational"—sensational in the sense that it "provokes excitement and interest" and becomes "a site of disturbance" (p. 19) in public discourses. Looking back, feminism and I grew closer and closer throughout this course as I engaged with a diverse set of perspectives based on anthropological, sociological, and feminist readings on families, parenting, childhood, childcare practices, single motherhood, LGBTQ parents, or sexuality. Perhaps I was engaged with my first feminist self-reflective practice: inherited notions restrict the imagination. It is where we are trapped within specific ways of seeing and understanding ourselves and the world around us. Feminism then becomes a 'sensational' process of unlearning these predetermined understandings. It is a practice of reimagining—a way to freely reimagine possibilities beyond such traps.

"Feminist work is often memory work," says Sara Ahmed in her book *Living a feminist life* (2017, p.22)— "to allow a memory to become distinct, to acquire a certain crispness or even clarity." Not remembering or remembering things without knowing what exactly they mean can be a 'symptom' of being trapped in something—in memories that are confusing, fragmented, and incomplete. When your memories are confusing, fragmented, and incomplete, it does something to your ability to tell your stories (Jackson, 2002), which becomes another trap, like a nightmare where you try to scream in rage, but no sound comes out. Thus, becoming a feminist is a 'constant struggle' (Davis, 2016) to remember your stories, connect them together, give them their clarity, regain your ability to tell them, and, finally, choose what stories you want to tell and how you tell them. When I started working on gender-based violence (GBV), or, to be exact, violence against women by men, for my PhD dissertation, it did not feel like a 'decision' I was taking—it was more like a feeling of being pushed towards a difficult topic, thick with emotions and sensations. I only realized later that it had begun as part of my own 'memory work,' not only to remember things as they were, but to find the words for what I experienced, make sense of them, acknowledge injustices they brought into my life, and to be able to recognize "how what happens to me, happens to others" (Ahmed, 2017, p. 27). While doing my fieldwork, I remember frequently finding myself imagining telling my stories of violence and harm—how I would tell them, how I would piece them together, what I would share, and how the imagined 'other'(s) might react. These imaginings stemmed from a desire to disclose the harm(s) inflicted, to speak up and 'complain,' and to be heard. It was a desire to transform "an individual harm to a collective one" (Fileborn, 2014, p. 44) by escaping the 'shameful' privacy of violence and creating a public voice. It was a desire to connect what is personal to political.

My memories of violence and harm personally connect me to feminism and help define it: they have shaped how I relate to the world around me. Roxane Gay, in an interview about her memoir Hunger (Meltzer, 2017), describes the experience of living in her body as being "trapped in a cage" and continues, "the frustrating thing about cages is that you're trapped, but you can see exactly what you want." Though always with a struggle, feminism is a way of extending my reach toward what I want, desire, and hope—I cannot undo what has been done, but I can 'overreact,' resist, defy, and risk (and own) being a 'killjoy' (Ahmed, 2017)—a bit of 'hysteric' and 'borderline.'

Finding Feminism as an Academic: Gender-based Violence Research in Turkey

In *Feminist Theory: From Margin to Center*, bell hooks (2015) defines feminism as a struggle—a movement and political commitment—to end sexism, sexist exploitation, and oppression. She further emphasizes that "its aim is not to benefit solely any specific group of women, any particular race or class of women" (p. 29). Feminism, particularly intersectional feminism, recognizes how sexism or sexist discrimination intersects with racism, class-based oppression, ageism, ableism, ethnic discrimination, and so forth (Crenshaw, 1991). In addition, the focus of any feminist theory is never solely individual, or as hooks (2015) highlights, "feminism is neither a lifestyle nor a ready-made identity or role one can step into" (p.29). Instead, feminism seeks the collective transformation of lives rather than focusing solely on individual change. Thus, feminist theory or research, as part of this broader feminist political commitment, always looks into how structures and systems of power uniquely operate and translate into oppression and vulnerability on a collective level.

My interest in feminism, while deeply connected to my personal story and has later evolved into a more general interest in feminism as a political movement, began and developed through my engagement with feminist theories—particularly standpoint feminism and feminist intersectionality—and by reading feminist psychology scholars such as Michelle Fine, Laura Brown, Lillian Comas-Díaz, Phyllis Chesler, and Jeanne Marecek. Thus, my engagement in feminist psychology research—or feminist research in general—and particularly in intersectional GBV research is a crucial part of how I relate to feminism. In a way, echoing scholars such as Fine (2012) and Lafrance & Wigginton (2019), I view my involvement in feminist intersectional GBV research as a form of advocacy work, as it seeks to expose and resist intersecting inequalities and oppression faced by GBV victim-survivors, and contribute to collective transformation through critical knowledge production and consciousness-raising. In what follows, I will first briefly define intersectional GBV research and then present two examples from my research practice.

Intersectional GBV research focuses on understanding how intersecting systems of oppression and discrimination (e.g., racism, sexism, classism, heteronormativity) constitute experiences of GBV (Crenshaw, 1991; Campbell & Mannell, 2016; Sokoloff & Dupont, 2005). Thus, rather than focusing on the intrapersonal and interpersonal dynamics of GBV, it emphasizes the broader structural and systemic realities that perpetuate and reinforce such violence. It focuses on the ongoing struggles of victim-survivors against societal and systemic constraints and highlights the role of social, political, and material inequalities in shaping their experiences of violence and vulnerability.

The first research example is based on my PhD study, which was transformative on a personal level as it intersected with my own journey into feminist thinking on violence, trauma, and mental health. The study focused on the decision-making and safety-seeking experiences of socioeconomically marginalized women in Turkey who were subjected to GBV in their marital relationships (Yalcinoz-Ucan, 2022). Therefore, it particularly speaks to the experiences of low-income urban women living in a conservative country where political determination and structural mechanisms to prevent and counteract violence are largely insufficient.

Feminism, both as a lens and a framework, was a critical component of this research study, enabling me to explore 'the possibilities of feminist research' (Fine, 1992) in order to develop a contextual understanding of women's responses to violence and experiences of trauma without pathologizing them. While trauma theory was initially grounded in feminist principles, as exemplified by Judith Herman's seminal work, *Trauma and Recovery* (1992), to understand and describe women's individual and collective experiences of suffering in relation to their subjugation to oppression, discrimination, exploitation, and abuse across interpersonal and structural contexts, its contemporary uses in psychology research and practice mostly describe and approach trauma primarily as a collection of 'symptoms' and a mental health issue rather than as a framework for analyzing the broader context and lived experiences that shape individual responses (Bryant-Davis, 2019; Tseris, 2013). Similarly, when GBV research relies on such decontextualized trauma perspectives, women's experiences of struggle in violent relationships are often reduced to a psychological issue primarily defined by the 'traumatic' impacts of violence (i.e., post-traumatic stress disorder, comorbid mental health challenges such as depression or anxiety).

Through feminist understandings of GBV and trauma in the context of this research, I was able to show how gender and class-based inequalities and barriers (i.e., poverty, unemployment, lack of material resources) intersect in women's experiences of GBV, fundamentally shaping their decisions and actions in violent relationships. Their stories addressed a broader oppressive political and societal system in Turkey, where their constant efforts to protect themselves were contextually constrained, constantly leaving them disempowered—both practically and emotionally—with limited individual power to 'take control' and escape violence.

Women's decision to stay in or leave violent relationships never reflects a binary decision, an individual or personal 'choice' between harm and safety or trauma and resilience because what is perceived as a simple personal act or decision is always situated within the structures: "The personal is structural" (Ahmed, 2017, p. 30). The experience of a young girl forcibly married to an adult man at the age of 15, enduring over a decade of violence, goes far beyond mere individual trauma; helplessness experienced by a woman who seeks help from the police but is ignored, dismissed, and sent back home cannot be explained as a psychological 'symptom' or consequence of trauma of violence; a woman's decision not to disclose violence, seek support, or leave in a context where poverty, unemployment, and housing insecurity are common does not indicate an 'avoidant' coping style or traumatic stress. Women's individual responses to violence—what they can or cannot do, how they feel, whether they speak out or remain silent, whether they stay or leave—are deeply shaped by the structural factors surrounding their lives. Structures reproduce violence and reinforce existing inequalities by denying women access to resources, protection, and justice.

Feminist theory and research as a 'praxis' helped me seek what is behind "the personal"—build connections between individual acts and structural forces, trauma and oppression, and helplessness and agency. Feminism found me in the stories of the women I interviewed and, at times, in their rightful anger toward my questions or assumptions. This happened, for example, when I asked a Kurdish Alevi woman 'why' she did not go to the police; her response ther have enough space nor feel equipped enough to accomplish such a task. Furthermore, by bringing them together, I do not naively suggest that they are without contradictions or entirely compatible with one another. Rather, I aim to reflect on my personal experiences of using them together as a psychotherapist despite their contradictions and incompatibilities.

Both feminism and psychoanalysis have profoundly shaped and transformed my relationship with myself, others, and the world. Asking feminist-psychoanalytic questions and engaging in feminist-psychoanalytic listening have disrupted many internalized cultural meanings I have held onto, expanded the reach of my understanding toward what is unknown, hidden, confusing, 'uncanny,' or fearful, and enabled new meanings, connections, and links. There had been times in my personal history when I could not put psychoanalysis and feminism together in my mind, and, thus, had made them enemies to each other—in a way, "attack[ed] the link" between them (Bion, 2013, p. 284) as if they could not survive together. Writing this reflection then feels like an act of reparation or reconciliation, an effort to 'link' them together.

One key way I see the link between psychoanalysis and feminism is that they both teach how to "bear witness to the chaos of people's lives so that they might find a way into the poetry of their experience" (Taylor, 2013, p. 28). Witnessing requires closely listening to the other's experience, meeting their vulnerability, pain, and suffering. Bearing witness to the other's chaos is no straightforward act. It first requires the witness's willingness and ability to face, recognize, and connect with their own chaos. Moreover, it requires a relationship, an attuned relatedness, in which "a dramatic dialogue" can be co-constructed and enacted (Atlas & Aron, 2017). This dialogue necessitates a simultaneous sense of mutuality and separateness on the part of the person who does the witnessing, a position simultaneously close and distant. While the witness should be in a position close enough to the other's chaos to allow themselves to be intimately touched by it, they must also be in a space distant enough to see possibilities beyond the chaos. It is to invite the other to 'dream' together (Ogden, 2017), co-create poetry in a 'facilitating environment' (Winnicott, 1971)—a dream and poetry that transform chaos into clarity, cohesion, and meaning (Taylor, 2013).

Neither psychoanalysis nor feminism prescribes a simple path to 'healing' or promises 'happiness' (Ahmed, 2010) in the conventional sense of escaping loss and pain (Brown, 2004; Ogden, 2017). Instead, both demand a painful working through of our individual and collective pasts. Healing, then, is not about pleasant, 'feel-good' moments or leaving everything behind (Taylor, 2013). Psychoanalysis and feminism, in their unique ways, offer us possibilities to become conscious of how our lives can be inhabited by unfairness, injustice, violence, hostility, and destruction; how we can feel alienated, deprived, and vulnerable by these; and how these realities then can damage our connection with the world, others, and ourselves. We can become blind to our pain and loss—just like becoming blind to racist, sexist, classist, heterosexist, and other forms of oppression surrounding our lives, trapped in the dynamics of 'doer and done-to' (Benjamin, 2018), losing our mutuality, spontaneity, and sense of freedom to feel and think. Through a demanding yet creative 'memory work' (Ahmed, 2017), psychoanalysis and feminism can show us then how it feels to have the freedom to feel and think. This crucial sense of 'freedom,' while we still mourn and bear our vulnerability, can simply give us the opportunity for playfulness in a Winnicottian sense—a "generative" playfulness (Atlas & Aron, 2017)—through which one can freely explore meanings and allow herself to dream and desire a 'better' future (Kagan, 2007), both individual and collective.

'Playing' as a creative experience—the ability to play—requires a 'facilitating' environment, a holding one (Winnicott, 1971). It is how I experience psychoanalysis and feminism, both as a facilitating environment, both offering me spaces to explore new ways of relating to myself and others through "spontaneity, freedom, and expressiveness [which] are joined dialectically with thoughtfulness, reflection, and creative choreography" (Atlas & Aron, 2017, p. 19). However, one could still ask: Does the world change when we change our relationship with ourselves? Another follow-up question could be: What happens to our ability to play, to our sense of generative playfulness, to our creativity and spontaneity, when the world stays the same? My understanding of 'the world' here is not a world 'facilitating' and 'enabling' but a world that generates injustice, exclusion, hostility, and harm—a world experienced by a child in a war zone, a world experienced by a refugee mother, a world experienced by a transwoman, a world experienced by a person with a wheelchair. Thus, the question is how 'playing' or 'symbolism' could be negotiated and maintained when the world continues to be a home for political violence and socio-cultural traumas (Tummala-Narra, 2022; Kagan, 2007).

None of these questions has straightforward answers, especially in the domain of psychotherapy. There is no easy path from individual to collective action and from personal to social change (Brown, 2004). The path is 'bumpy' (Ahmed, 2017)—messy and complex, far from being smooth and glossy. In grappling with such complexities, Tummala-Narra (2022) highlights the importance of adopting a therapeutic position or perspective beyond 'all-or-none' thinking that leads to conceptualizations of sociocultural context as "determining either everything or nothing about one's personality" (p. 228). This crucial insight aligns with what Chodorow (2019) calls 'both/and' approach rather than 'either/or'—meaning that neither seeing all "troubles and opportunities as coming from without" nor being stuck in an omnipotent fantasy by seeing "the world created from within" (Chodorow, 2019, p. 234). From a similar standpoint, Taylor (2013, p.31) reflects on her feminist therapy practice, asking, "Do I listen for critical connections to broader and more densely woven discourses of power and oppression in a client's expression of anger, or do I only hear symptoms or 'pathology'? Can I make room to hear both?"

Navigating internal and external realities simultaneously while listening to the multiplicity in the other's voice and stories requires an interpersonal space grounded in a depressive position. This is a space where "an overwhelming reality" can be processed without "the deadening of the inner life" (Kagan, 2007, p. 193) and where the symbolism of the inner life can be explored without denying or undermining external reality. Tummala-Narra (2022) argues that such a space can only be achieved through the therapist's recognition of the limits of psychotherapeutic work, on the one hand, and efforts to continue working through the unjust, traumatic, and sometimes life-threatening realities of the external world, on the other. She further suggests that these efforts, besides facilitating mourning, also foster:

> ... hope that is not based on false promises of equality and justice, but one that is based on the therapist naming the truth about sociocultural trauma and injustice, and recognizing that sociocultural trauma impacts the therapist and the patient in unique ways and that engaging with sociocultural trauma in psychotherapy can be painful and re-traumatizing to the patient and/or the therapist (Tummala-Narra, 2022, p. 230).

Ilany Kagan (2007), *in The Struggle against Mourning,* shares the case of Jacop, a client in psychoanalysis with whom she worked under the threat of war. Her client, at one point, strikingly remarks: "Out there, things are on fire, and we are sitting here discussing the fine nuances of feelings. It's such an indulgence! It's sociopathic, egocentric!" (p. 192). In her discussion of the case, Kagan reflects on her insistence on prioritizing the client's inner world as a purposeful effort to create "a sense of safety, to confirm the continuity of normal life, and to ensure the survival of both psychic and physical reality" (p. 194). She then criticizes her analytical approach, addressing how the denial of external reality "in the service of normality" (p. 192) diminished her empathic stance toward the client's realistic fears and concerns for his and his family's safety, disrupting her capacity to contain and transform them. She reports that her acknowledgment of these safety fears, by simply telling her client, "It is indeed very frightening to be here with little children during such times" (p. 191), became a turning point for the analysis. She emphasizes that only after this acknowledgment could her client see her as an 'ally,' which enabled him to process his internal and external conflicts simultaneously.

Still, despite the possibilities of psychotherapy linking internal with the external and engaging with sociopolitical traumas, one might ask: How relevant is psychotherapy in this sociopolitical context of inequality, violence, and destruction, especially if it cannot provide solutions to these real-world problems? Alternatively, as provocatively asked by Altman (2021, p. 59), "How do these real-world social dynamics [referring to politics, race, power, and white privilege] relate to one person paying high fees to lie on a couch and free associate, while another person sits behind the couch and interprets sexual and aggressive fantasies?" These are crucial and valid questions, particularly when we consider how psychotherapy or psychoanalysis, as institutionalized practices, may—whether through deliberate alignment with these systems or inadvertently due to ignorance or a lack of critical reflection—reinforce capitalist, patriarchal, colonial, and racist ideologies and discourses (Gordon-Brown et al., 2022; Parker & Pavón-Cuéllar, 2021). However, I will stop here as a fair discussion of these points requires a separate chapter of its own.

Conclusion

To conclude this chapter, I want to turn to Sara Ahmed one more time: "I think of feminist action as like ripples in water, a small wave, possibly created by agitation from weather; here, there, each movement making another possible, another ripple, outward, reaching. Feminism: the dynamism of making connections" (2016, p. 3). This is how I see my work as a feminist, researcher, and psychoanalytic psychotherapist. Making connections, both inside and outside the therapy room or academia, linking pieces together that once felt fragmented, making sense of what once did not make sense, pushing hard both inward and outward to extend the reach of understanding—all of these can begin with a single person, two people, a group of three, four, and so on, sitting in a room, starting to ask questions that have not been asked before. The world, for most people and most of the time, continues to be unaccommodating, disabling, or disempowering, yet we can always create room for agency, hope, desire, and resistance. We can find such rooms in psychoanalysis, feminism, and academia.

References

Ahmed, S. (2010). *The promise of happiness*. Durham and London: Duke University Press. https://doi.org/10.1215/9780822392781
Ahmed, S. (2017). *Living a feminist life*. Duke University Press. https://doi.org/10.2307/j.ctv11g9836
Ahmed, S. (2021). *Complaint!* Duke University Press. https://doi.org/10.1215/9781478022336
Altman, N. (2021). *White privilege: Psychoanalytic perspectives* (1st ed.). Routledge.
Atlas, G., & Aron, L. (2017). *Dramatic dialogue: Contemporary clinical practice* (1st ed.). Routledge. https://doi.org/10.4324/9781315150086

Benjamin, J. (2018). *Beyond doer and done to: Recognition theory, intersubjectivity and the third*. Routledge/Taylor & Francis Group.
Bion, W. R. (2013). Attacks on linking. *The Psychoanalytic Quarterly, 82*(2), 285–300. https://doi.org/10.1002/j.2167-4086.2013.00029.x
Brown, L. S. (2004). Feminist paradigms of trauma treatment. *Psychotherapy: Theory, Research, Practice, Training, 41*, 464–471. https://doi.org/10.1037/0033-3204.41.4.464
Bryant-Davis, T. (2019). The cultural context of trauma recovery: Considering the posttraumatic stress disorder practice guideline and intersectionality. *Psychotherapy, 56*(3), 400–408. https://doi.org/10.1037/pst0000241
Campbell, C., & Mannell, J. (2016). Conceptualising the agency of highly marginalised women: Intimate partner violence in extreme settings. *Global public health, 11*(1-2), 1–16. https://doi.org/10.1080/17441692.2015.1109694
Chodorow, N. (2019). *The psychoanalytic ear and the sociological eye: Toward an American independent tradition* (1st ed.). Routledge.
Crenshaw, K. (1991). Mapping the margins: Intersectionality, identity politics, and violence against women of color. *Stanford Law Review, 43*(6), 1241–1299. https://doi.org/10.2307/1229039
Davis, A. Y. (2016). *Freedom is a constant struggle: Ferguson, Palestine, and the foundations of a movement*. Haymarket Books.
Davids, T., & Willemse, K. (2014). Embodied engagements: Feminist ethnography at the crossing of knowledge production and representation — An introduction. *Women's Studies International Forum*, 43:1-4. https://doi.org/10.1016/j.wsif.2014.02.001
Fileborn, B. (2014). Online activism and street harassment: Digital justice or shouting into the ether? *Griffith Journal of Law & Human Dignity* 2(1): 32–51. https://doi.org/10.69970/gjlhd.v2i1.569
Fileborn, B. (2017). Justice 2.0: Street harassment victims' use of social media and online activism as sites of informal justice. *The British Journal of Criminology, 57*(6), 1482–1501.
Fine, M. (1992). Coping with rape: Critical perspectives on consciousness. In M. Fine (Ed.), *Disruptive voices: The possibility of feminist research* (pp. 61-76). The University of Michigan Press.
Fine, M. (2012). Troubling calls for evidence: A critical race, class and gender analysis of whose evidence counts. *Feminism & Psychology, 22*(1): 3–19. https://doi.org/10.1177/0959353511435475
Freeman, J. (1975). Political organization in the feminist movement. *Acta Sociologica, 18*(2-3), 222-244.
Gordon-Brown, C., Holmes, N., Kita, B., & Layton, L. (2022). Psychoanalytic spaces, implicated places. In R. Kabasakalian-McKay & D. Mark (Eds.), *Inhabiting implication in racial oppression and in relational psychoanalysis* (pp. 78-99). Routledge. https://doi.org/10.4324/9781003265146
Herman, J. L. (1992). *Trauma and recovery*. Basic Books/Hachette Book Group.
hooks, b. (2015). *Feminist theory: From margin to center* (3rd ed.). Routledge.
Jackson, M. (2002). *The politics of storytelling: Violence, transgression, and intersubjectivity* (Vol. 3). Museum Tusculanum Press.
Kagan, I. (2007).*The struggle against mourning*. Jason Aronson.
Klein, M. (1937). Love, guilt and reparation. In M. Klein (Ed.), *Love, guilt and reparation and other works 1921-1945* (pp. 306-343). The Free Press.

Lafrance, M. N., & Wigginton, B. (2019). Doing critical feminist research: A feminism & psychology reader. *Feminism & Psychology, 29*(4), 534–552. https://doi.org/10.11 77/0959353519863075

Loney-Howes, R. (2020). *Online anti-rape activism: Exploring the politics of the personal in the age of digital media.* Emerald Publishing Limited. https://doi.org/10.1108/978 1838674397

Meltzer, M. (2017, June 14). Roxane Gay's new memoir about her weight may be her most feminist-and revealing-act yet. *Elle.* https://www.elle.com/culture/a45920/roxane-gay-profile-hunger-memoir/

Nanditha, N. (2022). Exclusion in #MeToo India: Rethinking inclusivity and intersectionality in Indian digital feminist movements. *Feminist Media Studies, 22*(7), 1673–1694. https://doi.org/10.1080/14680777.2021.1913432

Ogden, T. H. (2017). Dreaming the analytic session: A clinical essay. *The Psychoanalytic quarterly, 86*(1), 1–20. https://doi.org/10.1002/psaq.12124

Parker, I., & Pavón-Cuéllar, D. (2021). *Psychoanalysis and revolution: Critical psychology for liberation movements.* 1968 Press.

Powell, A. (2015). Seeking rape justice: Formal and informal responses to sexual violence through technosocial counter-publics. *Theoretical Criminology, 19*(4), 571–588. https://doi.org/10.1177/1362480615576271

Rice, C. (2009). Imagining the other? Ethical challenges of researching and writing women's embodied lives. *Feminism & Psychology, 19*(2): 245-266. https://doi.org/10.1177/0959353509102222

Salter, M. (2013). Justice and revenge in online counter-publics: Emerging responses to sexual violence in the age of social media. *Crime, Media, Culture: An International Journal, 9*(3), 225–242. https://doi.org/10.1177/1741659013493918

Sokoloff, N. J., & Dupont, I. (2005). Domestic violence at the intersections of race, class, and gender: challenges and contributions to understanding violence against marginalized women in diverse communities. *Vilence Against Women, 11*(1), 38–64. https://doi.org/10.1177/1077801204271476

Taylor, S. (2013). Acts of remembering: Relationship in feminist therapy. *Women & Therapy, 36*(1-2), 23-34. https://doi.org/10.1080/02703149.2012.720498

Tseris, E. J. (2013). Trauma theory without feminism? Evaluating contemporary understandings of traumatized women. *Affilia, 28*(2), 153-164. https://doi.org/10.1177/088 6109913485707

Tummala-Narra, P. (2022). Can we decolonize psychoanalytic theory and practice? *Psychoanalytic Dialogues, 32*(3), 217–234. https://doi.org/10.1080/10481885.2022.20 58326

Tuzcu, P. (2016). "Allow access to location?" Digital feminist geographies. *Feminist Media Studies, 16*(1), 150–163. https://doi.org/10.1080/14680777.2015.1093153

Winnicott, D. W. (1971). *Playing and reality.* Penguin Books.

Yalcinoz-Ucan, B. (2022). Seeking safety from male partner violence in Turkey: Toward a context-informed perspective on women's decisions and actions. *Feminism & Psychology, 32*(4), 501-519. https://doi.org/10.1177/09593535221085497

Yalcinoz-Ucan, B., & Eslen-Ziya, H. (2023). Disclosing gender-based violence online: strengthening feminist collective agency or creating further vulnerabilities? *Feminist Media Studies, 24*(5), 1186–1203. https://doi.org/10.1080/14680777.2023.2229060

Yalcinoz-Ucan, B., & Eslen-Ziya, H. (2024). Online disclosure, a mechanism for seeking informal justice? *Crime, Media, Culture, 20*(1), 20-39. https://doi.org/10.1177/17416590231153077

Feminist Psychotherapies in Addressing Violence against Women

Leyla Soydinç

Mor Çatı (Purple Roof) Women's Shelter Foundation, Istanbul, Türkiye

The mainstream theoretical framework in the realm of psychological trauma has historically been built upon male norms and experiences, until feminist interventions challenged it. This construction has often rendered women's experiences invisible, excluded, and at times distorted, shaping the gender politics of psychological -well-being. However, particularly since the 1970s, the global influence of the second-wave feminist movement has revealed the gendered aspects of theory in the field of psychology, especially psychological trauma, leading to a perspective that transforms theoretical and practical approaches by critiquing methods that reference patriarchal norms. In psychological studies, the feminist approach has criticized research, theory and practice methods that use patriarchal norms as a reference point, excluding the experiences of those outside these norms.

The Historical Process of Gender in Spirituality: A Quote from Herman—"A Forgotten History"

Studies on psychological trauma—particularly in terms of theories, diagnoses, and treatment approaches—were predominantly shaped around men's combat experiences until the late 19th century, with the exception of the study of hysteria. Especially in the field of psychological trauma, studies were largely confined to men with war experiences until the feminist movement's intervention in the 1970s. However, research on hysteria became one of the few areas where women's experiences were prominently addressed. During these studies, it was discovered that the altered states of consciousness and emotional reactions defined as hysteria were often rooted in domestic violence and childhood abuse experienced by women (Herman, 1992).

    A key figure in the early study of hysteria was the French neurologist Jean-Martin Charcot, who focused on hysteria symptoms resembling neurological damage. He demonstrated that these symptoms could be artificially triggered and alleviated through hypnosis, proving their psychological origins. However, Charcot limited his focus to the symptoms themselves and did not delve into the experiences causing these conditions in his patients.

In the mid-1890s, Sigmund Freud, working independently but concurrently with Pierre Janet in France and Josef Breuer in Vienna, identified a similar phenomenon. They concluded that the condition labeled as hysteria was caused by psychological trauma. They argued that the unbearable emotional reactions stemming from traumatic events led to altered states of consciousness, giving rise to hysteria symptoms. As a treatment, they discovered that articulating traumatic memories could alleviate these symptoms. This therapeutic method laid the foundation for modern therapy. Janet referred to the technique as "psychological analysis," while Breuer and Freud called it "catharsis" or "talking cure." Freud later renamed the method as "psychoanalysis."

While conducting therapy sessions with women exhibiting hysteria symptoms, Freud often heard accounts of sexual violence and childhood abuse. In his 1896 study titled *The Aetiology of Hysteria*, based on 18 cases, Freud asserted that every case of hysteria had one or more incidents of childhood sexual abuse or violence at its root. However, within a year, Freud secretly abandoned this theory of the traumatic origins of hysteria. He feared the societal implications of exposing sexual violence and childhood abuse not only among the working class of Paris, where he initially conducted his research, but also among the bourgeois families of Vienna. Consequently, Freud stopped listening to his female patients.

For the next century, dominant psychological theories denied women's realities (Herman, 1981; Masson, 1984; Rush, 1977). Although sexuality remained a central focus of psychological research, the societal context of these experiences, especially their violent aspects, was ignored. Psychoanalysis shifted to a theory centered on the internal fluctuations of desire and fantasy, severed from the social reality of individual experiences. These interpretations went so far as to frame women's experiences of abuse and violence as manifestations of their sexual desires or fantasies (Freud, 1963; Lewis, 1976; Rose, 1985). This reality, described by Herman as "a forgotten history," was revived through the intervention of the feminist movement.

In the 1970s, during what is known as the second-wave feminist movement, feminists questioned the adequacy of addressing women's inequality and discrimination solely in the "public sphere" and called for politics to focus on the systemic male violence women faced in the "private sphere," such as within the home. At this juncture, "Consciousness-Raising Groups" played a pivotal role in steering politics in this direction and served as an inspirational model for psychological trauma studies.

Emerging in the late 1960s in the United States, these leaderless and non-hierarchical groups provided a space for women to share diverse experiences of womanhood, helping participants feel less isolated and offering supportive group dynamics. These groups enabled women to realize the systemic nature of the male violence they faced and, most importantly, to recognize that they were subjected to this violence not because of personal reasons but simply because they were women. For women, understanding that they were neither responsible for nor guilty of the violence, and finding safe spaces to share their emotions and experiences, were transformative. Although consciousness-raising groups were not initially intended as therapeutic spaces, their dynamics possessed a naturally healing quality. One of their most significant outcomes was the organization of political resistance against the violence women faced.

Feminist Psychoanalysis: A Historical Perspective

Understanding the conceptual background of feminist therapy requires examining the historical development of feminist psychoanalytic theories. Even without direct feminist influence, some of the patriarchal assumptions in Freud's works were recognized and criticized by his contemporaries. However, these productive debates within early psychoanalysis were short-lived. From the 1940s onward, the mainstream psychoanalytic tradition became increasingly orthodox, strictly adhering to Freud's interpretations, which were both conformist and sexist.

A glaring blind spot in foundational psychoanalytic texts is the ambiguity surrounding women's roles and the silence on male violence against women. Women are present in these narratives solely as "erotic objects" or "objects of desire." There is no meaningful connection established between being an object of desire and being a subject of domination. It is striking that a theory so directly concerned with sexuality and violence hardly addresses rape, except as part of discussions on children's unconscious fears and fantasies or women's so-called inherent masochism (Özkazanç, 2013).

Notably, figures like Karen Horney emerged within early psychoanalytic theory, directly influenced by women's demands for liberation and equality. In her book *The Neurotic Personality of Our Time* (1999), Horney analyzed women's issues, such as their "overvaluation of love" and struggles with "autonomy," offering psychological and social insights. She also provided social interpretations of concepts like penis envy and castration anxiety.

Later, theorists such as Julia Kristeva, Luce Irigaray, and Hélène Cixous paved the way for a different understanding of subjectivity by focusing on the pre-Oedipal stage and the relationship with the maternal body (the "maternal thing"). According to these thinkers, mainstream psychoanalytic theories exhibit violence by excluding women from subjectivity, reducing them to lack and deficiency and alienating them. They argue that this framework relies on a rigid philosophy of being and logic of sameness, suppressing the fluidity, relationality, and heterogeneity of human existence (Özkazanç, 2013).

With feminist interventions, the excluded subject—women's experiences—was finally included in the field of psychology. Moreover, this inclusion analyzed women's experiences within their social realities. Feminist psychologists aimed to uncover, redefine, conceptualize, and transform women's experiences, thereby linking them to the domain of mental health (Worell & Johnson, 1997).

Revisiting Suppressed and Distorted Experiences

Criticizing existing theories or introducing new ones required revisiting women's suppressed or distorted experiences through feminist research methods. This led to a renewed focus on issues like violence and childhood abuse. For example, a study conducted in the early 1980s by sociologist and human rights activist Diana Russell involving over 900 women revealed that one in four women had experienced rape and one in three had been sexually abused during childhood (Russell, 1984).

During this period, the feminist movement turned its attention to sexual violence. Feminists argued that rape was not about sexuality but a tool for demonstrating power and control over women, used to sustain male dominance (Brownmiller, 1975). This political stance not only exposed women's experiences of sexual violence but also highlighted its connection to patriarchy. It challenged myths that framed sexual violence as deviance and offered interpretations rooted in power dynamics. This shift provided a foundation for addressing sexual violence as a societal issue rather than an individual aberration, linking it to broader systems of power and control while amplifying the voices of women whose experiences had long been marginalized or ignored.

Male Violence and Its Effects on Women

After the systemic and pervasive nature of male violence against women in both public and private spaces was recognized, the direct link between this violence and the mental health challenges faced by women came into focus. The psychological effects of violence on women vary depending on the type of violence, its duration, severity, the life stage during which the violence occurs and the coping mechanisms and social support available to the individual. Feminist therapy holds particular significance in addressing the psychological health impacts of violence on women. This is because the source of violence against women is rooted in gender inequality, which is central to feminist therapy. The approach of feminist therapy is critical for women's processes of empowerment and recovery as they seek to distance themselves from violence or its effects. For this reason, the following section briefly explores the impact of violence against women on their psychological health.

The various forms of violence that women experience throughout their lives lead to restrictions on their lives, deprive them of the right to make decisions about their own lives, and weaken their sense of control over their lives. This has detrimental effects on both the physical and psychological health of women who experience violence. Initially, violence often elicits reactions such as shock or numbness. Over time, the fear of similar situations recurring may develop. In cases of chronic violence, women frequently experience feelings of insecurity, helplessness, hopelessness, a loss of control, self-blame and a decline in self-esteem (Stewart & Robinson, 1998). Prolonged exposure to violence can result in more complex psychological effects. Feelings of distrust towards oneself and the external world, as well as increased feelings of helplessness and hopelessness, may intensify. Women, especially when unable to stop the violence—something only the perpetrator can do—may begin to feel shame. The perpetrator's controlling behavior often limits women's communication and emotional sharing with others, leading to isolation. This sense of isolation may cause women to develop stronger emotional dependence on the perpetrator. Additionally, excessive control makes it more difficult for women to cope with the violence. In an attempt to cope, some women may normalize the violence by finding justifications for it or convince themselves that the situation is "not so bad" when they cannot stop it (Mor Çatı Women's Shelter Foundation, 2017). This can trap them in a cycle of violence. Similarly, women subjected to violence by their partners may convince themselves that they deserve the mistreatment because they are not obedient enough or are inadequate as partners.

The efforts of feminists to uncover such realities have contributed to the development of numerous concepts in psychological trauma studies. Psychologist Lenore Walker coined the term "battered woman syndrome," identifying common patterns of responses among women experiencing violence (Walker, 1979). According to Walker's cycle theory of violence, developed in 1979, women experiencing violence often go through three distinct phases. Although these phases do not occur in the same way in every relationship, many abusive relationships follow a pattern known as the "cycle of violence," which makes it difficult for women to escape the cycle. The phases of the cycle are: the tension-building phase, the acute violence phase, and the reconciliation or remorse phase. The effects of this cycle of violence on women are profound and long-lasting. During the tension-building phase, women experience heightened anxiety and fear as they attempt to avoid triggering the abuser, which erodes their sense of safety and self-worth. In the acute violence phase, the emotional and physical trauma inflicted can cause immediate harm, including injury, psychological distress, and a deep sense of helplessness. The reconciliation phase, while seemingly offering hope and relief, can further entrap the victim in a cycle of false promises and emotional manipulation, making it difficult to leave. This cyclical nature of abuse often leaves women feeling powerless, confused and isolated, making it harder for them to break free and seek help, as the abuser's remorseful behavior can momentarily mask the severity of the situation. Hopefully, the recently added "open-door phase" is a critical time when victims may have an opportunity to break free from the abusive cycle. Feminist interventions and therapy play a pivotal role in this phase by empowering the women with tools, insights and support to challenge the underlying gender inequalities that fuel the abuse.

From the 1970s and 1980s onward, studies also began to examine the mental health effects of sexual violence and childhood sexual abuse on women. In 1972, psychiatric nurse Ann Burgess and sociologist Lynda Holmstrom conducted a study on the psychological effects of rape (Burgess &Holmstorm, 1974). They observed a psychological reaction pattern in women subjected to rape, which they termed the "rape trauma syndrome." They noted that women generally experienced rape as a life-threatening event, fearing permanent injury or death during the assault. Women who experienced rape reported symptoms such as dissociation, numbness, insomnia, nausea, hypervigilance and nightmares. These symptoms were found to resemble those previously identified in combat veterans. The psychological study of domestic violence and child sexual abuse has also led to a rediscovery of trauma syndromes. Judith Herman's research revealed parallels between the psychology of incest survivors and late 19th-century observations of hysteria (Herman & Hirschman, 1977).

Research into the effects and prevalence of sexual violence and violence against women has been incorporated into psychiatric literature. According to a 2002 World Health Organization (WHO) report, the higher prevalence of mental illnesses among women is attributed more to their increased exposure to stress and risk factors than to biological predisposition. Campbell's (2002) study found that women exposed to psychological violence, in addition to physical and sexual violence, experienced similar mental health problems. Furthermore, women exposed to violence are at a higher risk of developing chronic depression (Karakoç et al., 2015). Studies have also shown that women's anxiety and depression levels decrease once they distance themselves from the violence and feel safe. Kessler and colleagues (1995) calculated the lifetime prevalence of exposure to traumatic events to be 10.4% for women and 5.0% for men. Researchers suggested that this gender difference is primarily due to women's higher likelihood of experiencing trauma caused by intentional acts of human violence (e.g., abuse, violence). Certain characteristics of

Feminist Psychotherapies in Addressing Violence against Women   33

traumatic events—such as intentional violence, life-threatening circumstances, physical injury, unpredictability, uncontrollability, sexual violence, or prolonged/repeated trauma—were identified as significantly associated with post-trauma effects (Briere & Scott, 2014). These characteristics strongly overlap with those of gender-based violence. The lifetime prevalence of PTSD among women exposed to sexual violence ranges from 32% to 80% (Resnick et al., 1993). Another longitudinal study found that 44-66% of women who experienced violence continued to exhibit PTSD symptoms for up to nine years after separating from their partners (Anderson et al., 2003). Furthermore, physical and sexual violence, which violates women's bodily boundaries, negatively affects their body image (Harned, 2000).

Experiencing violence is a significant risk factor for psychological trauma. Women subjected to violence are at risk of developing PTSD, major depressive disorder, generalized anxiety disorder, panic disorder, somatoform disorder, dissociative disorders, substance use disorders, and adjustment disorders (Yüksel, 2012). Numerous studies also indicate a negative correlation between partner violence and self-esteem (Aguilar & Nightingale, 1994; Cascardi & O'Leary, 1992). Women who reported experiencing violence also frequently mentioned issues with fear, anxiety, and difficulties in forming close relationships (Bengtsson-Tops & Tops, 2007). Victims of sexual violence may perceive their bodies as vulnerable or a source of shame due to victim-blaming attitudes and gender stereotypes, attributing the cause of the violence to their physical appearance and feeling guilty (Kearney-Cooke & Striegel-Moore, 1994).

As evident from these findings, it is crucial to understand women's psychological health challenges not through essentialist explanations that attribute them to biology but by examining the systemic discrimination and violence rooted in gender-based power imbalances. However, it is important to note that not all women subjected to violence experience mental health difficulties or trauma in the same way. Various factors—such as the type, intensity, and frequency of violence—affect its impact. Additionally, women's internal and external support systems, resilience and capacity for mental endurance must not be overlooked. All women subjected to any form of violence can recover and lead fulfilling lives. Nevertheless, the fight against the system of gender inequality that hinders this recovery process continues. Feminist therapy focuses on addressing and challenging this system in both clinical settings and therapeutic spaces.

From Theory to Practice: Feminist Psychotherapy

Feminists have drawn attention to advocacy in social action and public policies by developing critical theoretical approaches to the realm of mental health and creating new research methods to make women's experiences visible in therapeutic practices. They have brought innovative and transformative perspectives to therapeutic practices by developing new research methods to make women's experiences visible, and by drawing attention to advocacy in social action and public policies (Worell, 2000). With the "personal is political" awareness that emerged with the second-wave feminist movement, it became possible to address issues such as male violence, power relationships, and gender roles in both theoretical and individual practice fields of psychology. Feminist therapy emerged by focusing on the fundamental debates and principles of the feminist movement. The conceptualization and method of feminist therapy are based on consciousness-raising groups mentioned in the previous section and the efforts of feminist therapists to bring the political principles of feminism into the therapy room (Brown, 1994; Brown & Brodsky, 1992).

The impact of feminist therapy has expanded significantly in the last 40 years. As feminist theory deepened its analysis of gender, power, and social positions, feminist therapists expanded their work to a wide range of issues. It would not be entirely appropriate to say that feminist therapy is its own school of therapy. Feminist therapy is an approach that can be applied with various approaches and practices. The question of whether any therapy can be considered a feminist practice can be answered by examining whether the therapy supports feminist change models and discusses the impact of social factors and patriarchy on psychological well-being (Brown, 2010). However, feminist therapists have certainly conducted studies on how feminist therapy can be conducted in collaboration with other therapy approaches. These studies were conducted by Laura Brown (2010) and included cognitive therapies (Davis & Padesky, 1989; Diaz-Martinez et al., 2010; Worell & Remer, 2002), gestalt therapy (Enns, 1987), psychoanalytic therapies (Alpert, 1986; Benjamin, 1998; Goldner, 2002; Luepnitz, 1988, 2003; Toronto et al., 2005; Tummala-Narra, 2016), family systems therapies (Hare-Mustin, 1978; McGoldrick, 1998; Silverstein & Goodrich, 2003), psychodrama (Worell & Remer, 2002), and EMDR therapy (Brown, 2002). Various models have already internalized feminist structures for the treatment of individuals experiencing complex trauma (Courtois, 2000; Gold, 2000; Harvey, 1996; Harvey & Tummala-Narra, 2007), as the concept of complex trauma was initially formulated in feminist research and clinical interventions for individuals who have endured sexual violence, as proposed by Herman and her colleagues in their 1992 work.

The Therapeutic Process of Feminist Psychotherapy

Equal and Empowering Relationship between Client and Therapist

At the core of feminist therapy lies an egalitarian and empowering relationship between the client and the therapist. The interpersonal context of therapy is seen as the place where the idea of empowerment takes shape (Brown, 1994; Faunce, 1985; Greenspan, 1983; Smith & Siegel, 1985). However, achieving this equality in therapy practice is structurally challenging due to institutional roles and laws that surround it. An egalitarian relationship in therapy does not mean unrealistic elimination of hierarchy or complete equalization of positions. Instead, it is based on the idea that each client deserves equal value. It recognizes each client as an expert, bringing specific skills and knowledge to the therapeutic relationship, with no expertise being more valuable than another. Feminist therapy acknowledges the structural asymmetry in the therapeutic relationship and utilizes systemic strategies within legal and ethical norms to minimize this asymmetry as much as possible in the therapist's affiliated therapeutic practice (Brown, 2010).

When defining the parameters of egalitarian and empowering dynamics, attention should be paid to how the social privileges of both parties enter the psychotherapeutic domain (Halley, 2011; Kimmel, 2009; McIntosh, 1998). Privilege highlights the systematic provision of unearned advantages, such as power, access to resources, and protection from harm, to individuals occupying specific social positions. Privilege is not earned and is not distributed equally. Therefore, an individual's privilege may function to intentionally or unintentionally suppress or disempower others. Since everyone has intersecting identities such as ethnic identity, gender, age, and sexual orientation, most people have complex experiences of privilege. Hence, the theory of feminist therapy is based on exploring and analyzing how both individuals' power and privilege manifest in the therapy encounter, both outside and within the therapy session. Undiscovered privilege weakens the goal of an egalitarian and empowering therapeutic relationship. Feminist therapists collaborate with clients on therapy goals, working together to determine them. To establish such collaboration, the client and therapist must focus on exploring the client's desires, the reality of the conditions, and the boundaries of the therapist's expertise. This collaboration requires taking into account the client's readiness levels, stages of change, and willingness to address any issue or problem (Brown, 2010).

Addressing Themes of Gender Inequality

Feminist therapists argue that traditional therapeutic methods fall short in addressing violence and discrimination against women and advocate for the integration of feminist approaches. To effectively address the mental health issues experienced by women, the therapeutic process must consider not only personal dynamics but also the societal context (Evans et al., 2011). Therefore, all beliefs and values in the therapeutic process should be connected to gender roles, power relationships, cultural norms, and power dynamics.

In feminist therapy, all issues are approached, analyzed, and worked on within the context of one's gender, power relationships, and the power system. However, this does not mean that the therapist takes on a didactic role, teaches, or positions themselves as superior. The therapist merely opens up space for the client to think about or question their experiences within this context. Feminist therapy aims to establish connections between hidden aspects related to gender roles, the difficulties individuals face, and the relationship between these challenges and power dynamics. It assists individuals in recognizing these aspects and exploring possibilities and alternatives for forming different types of relationships (Polat-Işık et al., 2019).

Working with the Dynamics of Violence and Challenging Myths about Violence

Some traditional theories analyzing violence against women in the field of psychological health completely overlook the societal dimension of violence and attribute it solely to personal dynamics. Before the analyses offered by feminist perspectives, mainstream approaches explained violence against women as the result of the "psychological imbalance of a few men," focusing more on psychological processes than societal contexts.

Early research, even conducted within traditional methods, challenges the thesis that the majority of men who commit violence have psychological problems. For example, in 1978, only 3.5% of rape offenders were placed under hospital supervision under mental health law (Walby, 1990). The belief that violence against women is due to "the psychological imbalance of a few men" cannot adequately explain this societal issue. Similarly, the widespread belief that violence against women is caused by men's anger is also critiqued from a feminist perspective. Choosing to use violence is a preference and men choose this behavior to demonstrate power and control over women. Explaining violence in terms of psychological illness or anger control issues pathologizes violence and obscures the responsibility of the person committing violence.

Likewise, there are numerous societal myths about sexual violence that normalize or legitimize it. The most common is the belief that committing sexual violence is related to the inability to control sexual urges. Sexual violence is not a form of sexuality; it is the use of violence as a tool to control, manipulate, demean, humiliate, and punish women. From a feminist perspective, sexual violence is an act of violence aimed at "putting women in their place" and serves as a mechanism of social control (Scully, 2013).

Additionally, another widespread myth about violence against women is that socio-economic status determines the perpetration or victimization of violence. However, it is known that men can commit violence at all levels of education and income. The only meaningful difference is that as education levels increase, men tend to use more professional methods of violence, such as psychological violence and manipulation, rather than physical violence. Women can be subjected to violence at any education and income level because being subjected to male violence is related to being a woman. However, education and economic status can be determinants of access to resources and support for women subjected to violence. Apart from that, it cannot be presented as a reason for being subjected to violence.

In conclusion, the reason men commit violence against women is to control, monitor, and display power. Therefore, committing violence is a consequence of unequal power relationships created by societal gender roles and the patriarchal system that reproduces them. Therefore, in psychological support work with women subjected to violence, discussing the dynamics of violence, its systematic nature, gender relationships, the cycle of violence, myths about violence, and the impact of violence on women is an essential part of feminist therapy. Of course, these themes are addressed in the therapy process based on the flow of the therapy, the readiness of the woman, and the pace at which she is comfortable. Discussing violence in this context opens up space for women to make sense of the violence they experience, talk about emotions such as guilt, helplessness, shame, and discuss feelings of hope, believing that the person who uses violence can change. Therapists working with a feminist approach focus on empowering their clients and supporting them in taking control of their lives. The main point of the therapeutic relationship is to support the client in the process of self-discovery (Chaplin, 1999).

Support Client's Connection with Resources

In feminist therapy, clients may have weakened relationships with both internal and external resources due to gender inequality and experiences of discrimination and/or violence based on their lived gender. Therefore, in feminist therapy, it is crucial to connect clients with relevant resources when their current needs are identified. For example, if a woman seeking psychological support due to experiencing violence is found to need social or legal support, information about social and legal support channels is provided, along with details about places where she can engage in solidarity relationships (Eyüpoğlu, 2008). Hence, it should be acknowledged that feminist therapy is intertwined with social work. However, to avoid creating role conflict, it is important to share essential information with the client, establish boundaries in the therapy, and not exceed guidance and/or collaboration with other experts.

"Self-disclosure" in Feminist Therapy

Feminist therapists utilize a range of structural and ecological strategies in their practice to highlight the shared experiences among individuals (e.g., female therapist-female client) stemming from gender inequality and to reduce power imbalances. However, none of these methods are mandatory for a feminist therapist. Research on "self-disclosure" in the therapeutic relationship (Hill & Knox, 2002; Tsai et al., 2017) and the value placed on therapist authenticity in person-centered models (Rogers, 1957) align with the idea that a feminist therapist's self-disclosure can be a strategy used for empowering clients (Brown & Brodski, 1992; Feminist Therapy Institute, 1990, 1999).

Feminist therapy asserts that there is no "neutral" or "objective" therapist, and the concept of supposed neutrality often perpetuates the perspective of the person with the most power. Therefore, therapists can choose not to explicitly disclose their feminist beliefs, sexual orientations, or social class backgrounds. However, therapists should be mindful that such a decision to reduce personal vulnerability does not become a systemic move away from an egalitarian stance (Brown, 2010).

In feminist therapy, more indirect strategies can be developed for self-disclosure. For example, working with women who have experienced violence, expressing shared anger when a client observes the injustices in the legal process can be a method of self-disclosure within certain boundaries. At times, linguistic maneuvers can also be employed for self-disclosure. For instance, when working with a woman who has experienced violence, occasionally shifting to the "we" language, such as saying, "as women, we experience various forms of violence," can convey to the client that the female therapist sees herself as a subject, not immune to violence, in solidarity with the client.

Self-reflection of the Feminist Therapist

In all psychotherapies, it is essential for therapists to reflect on and work on themselves, going through their own therapy and supervision processes. However, in feminist therapy, it is critically important for the therapist to confront their own gender patterns and biases. For instance, if a therapist working with a woman experiencing violence and unable to leave an abusive relationship is feeling intense disappointment or getting angry at a woman who expresses unwillingness to take care of her child, the therapist needs to work on these judgments and emotions.

Despite our imagination, everyone is born into a gendered world and internalizes gender roles to some extent. Therefore, questioning oneself about gender roles is an ongoing process, not something that ends at a certain point, independent of one's education, expertise, and personal characteristics. A person claiming to be free from all gender biases may risk a weakening of insight into these biases. Thus, the process of questioning the therapist's gender stereotypes, perspectives, and language choices holds significance not only on a personal but also on a professional level.

"Personal is Political": The Therapy Room

The feminist movement has questioned, criticized, analyzed, and proposed various concepts and methods to transform all areas of the mental health tradition from its own perspective. Feminist therapy is unique among all application areas because it focuses on both personal and social change (Evans et al., 2011). However, this does not mean that feminism becomes an imposition or has a mandatory agenda in the therapy room. Psychological support work conducted through a feminist approach inherently leads to social transformation by connecting individual issues to social contexts and focusing on the influence of the gender system on mental well-being. While feminist therapy varies in application across different contexts and schools, any work that questions the gender system is both individual and social. In feminist therapy, individuals are provided with a space to question and contemplate their experiences, emotions, and mental health, including mental challenges, related to their gender. After these inquiries, the individual's unique process of reaching a conclusion and evolving is entirely unique and not subject to direction. From this perspective, feminist therapy is not just a technique but a revolutionary approach that includes both individual and social change theory (Williams, 1995).

In contemporary traditional therapy practices, it is observed that mainstream practices neglecting the social context of individual experiences and approaches reproducing gender roles particularly hinder individuals' healing processes in trauma work. Therefore, applying psychological support practices with feminist approaches opens up a way for individuals to be empowered, establishing a non-hierarchical solidarity relationship with them and organizing social transformation through these personal practices.

Feminist Psychological Support Work at Mor Çatı Women's Shelter Foundation: Solidarity with Women and Advocating for Change

Mor Çatı Women's Shelter Foundation was established in 1990 by feminists in order to combat violence against women. At Mor Çatı, the work against male violence is grounded in feminist principles, aiming for women to be able to build lives unhindered by gender-based discrimination and male violence in free and equal conditions. Male violence is understood to be rooted in existing inequalities between men and women, which must be dismantled by fostering women's solidarity. For this reason, the social work at our solidarity center and shelter is geared towards empowering women. In addition to engaging in one-on-one solidarity with women, Mor Çatı monitors and reports on the implementation of national and international conventions, laws, and regulations. The organization also makes policy recommendations to decision-makers in order to eradicate violence and achieve gender equality.

Within the framework of Mor Çatı, psychological support holds a pivotal role in establishing solidarity with women. This acknowledgment is rooted in an understanding of the profound impact of male violence on women's psychological well-being. Psychological support is positioned as a crucial component within Mor Çatı's comprehensive and holistic support work. Recognizing that women may require such support to distance themselves from violence or its lingering effects is central to Mor Çatı's approach. The difficulty of accessing psychological support, particularly from therapists with a feminist perspective in Turkey, is acknowledged. Mor Çatı emerges as a pivotal channel facilitating women's access to much-needed psychological support.

Framework for Feminist Psychological Support Work of Mor Çatı

Mor Çatı has implemented a structured framework for psychological support, usually consisting of 20 sessions over a period of six months. This flexible timeframe allows for personalized evaluations based on the unique needs of individual women. The purpose of this framework is twofold: it defines the boundaries of Mor Çatı's capacity and scope while offering a sense of structure to women who often contact the organization during moments of crisis or chaos—even in cases of non-acute violence, where its effects may still persist. Mor Çatı does not engage in clinical work and chooses to politically remain within the framework of solidarity, with a specific focus on the impact of violence.

Addressing the Accessibility Barrier

Unfortunately, access to psychological support remains limited in Turkey, especially for women who have experienced violence. Finding a therapist who works with a feminist perspective and understands the dynamics of violence is particularly challenging. To address this gap, Mor Çatı provides a channel for women who seek support.

This framework for support also reflects Mor Çatı's limitations as an organization. Mor Çatı is not a clinic, nor does it have the resources or mission to provide long-term psychotherapy. Instead, it focuses on addressing the impact of women's experiences with violence through psychological work that aligns with its feminist and policy-driven approach. This scope ensures that the organization can effectively establish solidarity with as many women as possible within its capacity while providing trauma and women-centered support.

A Feminist Framework for Psychological Work

Mor Çatı's psychological support is underscored by feminist principles, challenging societal myths and beliefs surrounding violence against women through targeted psychological interventions. Regardless of the therapeutic methods employed, the shared approach is feminist, aiming to build solidarity with women as they navigate away from violence and its effects. Central to this work is discussing the dynamics of violence—its roots in gender-based power imbalances and its impact on the psychology of women. What unites the team is the shared understanding that they work under the Mor Çatı umbrella, with a commitment to feminist principles. Women often arrive at Mor Çatı already aware of these principles, and this can lead to important discussions in therapy.

The Interconnection of Psychological and Social Work

Emphasizing the interconnectedness of psychological and social work, Mor Çatı illustrates how these two domains collaborate to offer holistic support to women facing violence. These two areas are in constant dialogue, enabling a multifaceted approach to supporting women. For example, while a psychologist may identify a woman's need for legal support, a social worker might recognize the necessity of psychological assistance and refer her accordingly. This collaboration aligns with feminist therapy's emphasis on reconnecting women with resources that violence has disrupted.

This integrated approach also extends to producing reports that support women during legal proceedings. Mor Çatı provides women with reports that support them during legal processes without diagnosing or evaluating their psychological state. While these reports do not diagnose or evaluate mental health, they provide observations on the impact of violence on women's lives. These reports can be particularly significant in cases such as divorce or custody disputes and sexual assault cases, where women frequently face accusations challenging their mental stability or parental competence, alongside pervasive victim-blaming.

Policy and Advocacy through Psychological Support

The scope of psychological support work at Mor Çatı extends beyond individual support, encompassing healing, empowerment and political action. Mor Çatı's approach to psychological support significantly contributes to the broader feminist movement and actively challenges societal norms related to violence against women. Through this support, Mor Çatı observes the emotional toll of violence on women and challenges societal myths that attribute the root of violence to issues like anger management or mental health disorders. These insights are documented and shared through workshops and meetings with psychologists and social workers, aiming to strengthen mechanisms for combating violence.

Ultimately, psychological support at Mor Çatı reflects the belief that the personal is political. By addressing the psychological impact of violence, Mor Çatı not only builds solidarity with women but also contributes to creating policies that challenge patriarchal structures and foster collective empowerment.

References

Aguilar, R.J., & Nightingale, N.N. (1994). The impact of specific battering experiences on the self-esteem of abused women. *Journal of Family Violence, 9*, 35–45.

Alpert, J. L. (Ed.). (1986). *Psychoanalysis and women: Contemporary reappraisals* (1st ed.). Routledge.

Anderson, D. K., Saunders, D. G., Yoshihama, M., Bybee, D. I., & Sullivan, C. M. (2003). Long-term trends in depression among women separated from abusive partners. *Violence against Women, 9*(7), 807-838.

Bengtsson-Tops, A. & Tops, D. (2007). Self-reported consequences and needs for support associated with abuse in female users of psychiatric care. *International Journal of Mental Health Nursing, 16*(1), 35-43.

Benjamin, J. (1998). Shadow of the Other: Intersubjectivity and Gender in *Psychoanalysis* (1st ed.). Routledge. https://doi.org/10.4324/9780203948149

Briere J. N., & Scott C. (2014). *Principles of trauma therapy: A guide for symptoms, assessment, and treatment updated for DSM-5*. Sage Publications.

Brown., L. S. (2002). Feminist therapy and EMDR: A theory meets a practice. In F. Shapiro (Ed.), *EMDR as an integrative psychotherapy approach: Experts of diverse orientations explore the paradigm prism* (pp. 263–287). Washington, DC: American Psychological Association. http://dx.doi.org/10.1037/10512-011

Brown, L. S. (1994). *Subversive dialogues: theory in feminist therapy*. New York, NY: Basic Books

Brown, L. S. (2010). *Feminist therapy*. American Psychological Association.

Brown, L. S., & Brodsky, A. M. (1992). The future of feminist therapy. *Psychotherapy: Theory, Research, Practice, Training*, 29(1), 51–57. https://doi.org/10.1037/0033-3204.29.1.51

Brownmiller, S. (1975). *Against our will: Men, women, and rape*. New York: Simon & Schuster.

Burgess A.W., & Holmstrom, L. L. (1974). Rape trauma syndrome. *American Journal of Psychiatry 131*(9), 981-986.

Campbell, A. (2002). *A mind of her own: The evolutionary psychology of women*. Oxford University Press.

Cascardi, M., & O'Leary, K. D. (1992). Depressive symptomatology, self-esteem, and self-blame in battered women. *Journal of Family, Violence, 7*, 249-259.

Chaplin, J. (1999). *Feminist counseling in action*. SAGE Pub.

Courtois, C. (2000). *Recollections of sexual abuse*. New York, NY: Norton.

Davis, D., & Padesky, C. (1989). Enhancing cognitive therapy with women. In A. Freeman, K. M. Simon, L. E. Beutler, & H. Arkowitz (Eds.) *Comprehensive Handbook of Cognitive Therapy*. Springer, New York, NY.

Diaz-Martinez, A., Interian, A., & Waters, D. (2010). The integration of CBT, multicultural, and feminist therapies with Latinas. *Journal of Psychotherapy Integration*, *20*(3), 312–326.
Enns, C. Z. (1987). Gestalt therapy and feminist therapy: A proposed integration. *Journal of Counseling & Development, 66*(2), 90-95.
Evans, K. M., Kincade, E. A., & Seem, S. R. (2011). Feminist therapy: A social and individual change model. *Introduction to feminist therapy: Strategies for social and individual change* (pp. 13-24). SAGE Publications.
Eyüpoğlu, H. (2008). Cinsel taciz ve travma: Eleştirel bir deneyim aktarımı [Sexual abuse and trauma: A critical account of experience]. *Eleştirel Psikoloji Bülteni*, (1), 61-68.
Faunce, P. S. (1985). A feminist philosophy of treatment. In L. B. Rosewater & L. E. A. Walker (Eds.), *Handbook of feminist therapy: Women's issues in psychotherapy* (pp. 1–5). New York, NY: Springer
Feminist Therapy Institute. (1990). Feminist Therapy Institute code of ethics. In H. Lerman & N. Porter (Eds.), *Feminist ethics in psychotherapy* (pp. 37–40). New York, NY: Springer.
Feminist Therapy Institute. (1999). *Feminist therapy institute code of ethics*. Denver, CO: Author.
Freud, S. (1963). *Dora: An analysis of a case of hysteria*. Collier Books, Macmillan Publishing.
Gold, S. N. (2000). *Not trauma alone*. Thousand Oaks, CA: Sage.
Goldner, V. (2002). Toward a critical relational theory of gender. In M. Dimen & V. Goldner (Eds.), *Gender in psychoanalytic space: Between clinic and culture* (pp. 63–90). Other Press.
Greenspan, M. (1983). *A new approach to women and therapy*. New York, NY: McGraw-Hill.
Halley, J. (2011). *Seeing White: An introduction to White privilege and race*. Lanham, MD: Rowman & Littlefield.
Hare-Mustin., R. T. (1978). A feminist approach to family therapy. *Family Process*, 17, 181–194. http://dx.doi.org/10.1111/j.1545- 5300.1978.00181.x
Harned M. S. (2000). Harassed bodies: An examination of the relationships among women's experiences of sexual harassment, body image, and eating disturbances. *Psychology of Women Quarterly*, *24*(4): 336- 348.
Harvey., M. R. (1996). An ecological view of psychological trauma and trauma recovery. *Journal of Traumatic Stress*, 9, 3–23. http://dx.doi.org/10.1002/jts.2490090103
Harvey., M. R., & Tummala-Narra, P. (2007). *Sources and expressions of resiliency in trauma survivors: Ecological theory, multicultural practice*. New York, NY: Routledge
Herman J. L., & Hirschman, L. (1977). Father-daughter incest. *Signs: Journal of Women in Culture and Society 2*(4), 735-756.
Herman, J. L. (1981). *Father-daughter incest*. Cambridge: Harvard University Press.
Herman, J. L. (1992). *Trauma and recovery: The aftermath of violence--from domestic abuse to political terror*. New York: Basic Books.
Hill., C., & Knox, S. (2002). Self-disclosure. In J. C. Norcross (Ed.), *Psychotherapy relationships that work: Therapist contributions and responsiveness to patients* (pp. 255–266). New York, NY: Oxford University Press.
Horney, K. (1999). *The neurotic personality of our time*. Routledge.

Karakoç B, Gülseren L, Çam, B., Gülseren, Ş., Tenekeci, N, & Mete, L. (2015). Prevalence of domestic violence and associated factors. *Neuro Psychiatry Archive. 52*(4), 324-330.

Kearney-Cooke, A. & Striegel-Moore, R. H. (1994). Treatment of childhood sexual abuse in anorexia nervosa and bulimia nervosa: A feminist psychodynamic approach. *International Journal of Eating Disorders. 15*(4):305-319.

Kessler, R. C., Sonnega, A., Bromet, E., Hughes, M., & Nelson, C. B. (1995). Posttraumatic stress disorder in the National Comorbidity Survey. *Arch Gen Psychiatry 52*(12):1048-60. doi: 10.1001/archpsyc.1995.03950240066012. PMID: 7492257.

Kimmel, M. (2009). *Privilege: A reader.* Boulder, CO: Westview Press.

Lewis, H. B. (1976). *Psychic war in men and women.* New York University Press.

Luepnitz, D. A. (1988). *The family interpreted: Feminist theory in clinical practice.* Basic Books.

Luepnitz, D. A. (2003). *Schopenhauer's porcupines: Intimacy and its dilemmas.* New York, NY: Basic Books.

Masson, J. M. (1984). *The assault on truth. Freud's suppression of the seduction theory.* New York: Farrar, Straus & Giroux.

McGoldrick, M. (1998). *Re-visioning family therapy: Race, culture, and gender in clinical practice.* New York, NY: Guilford Press.

McIntosh, P. (1998). White privilege: Unpacking the invisible knapsack. In M. McGoldrick (Ed.), *Re-visioning family therapy: Race, culture, and gender in clinical practice* (pp. 147–152). New York, NY: Guilford Press.

Mor Çatı Women's Shelter Foundation (2017). *Stand against men's violence! Change lives!* Istanbul.

Özkazanç, A. (2013). *Cinsellik, şiddet ve hukuk: Feminist yazılar.* Ankara: Dipnot Yayınları.

Polat-Işık, A. Ö., Sodan-Turan, H., & Kaynar-Keçeli, G. (2019). Kadınlarla yapılan araştırmalarda cinsiyet yanlılıkları ve yöntem sorunları [Gender biases and methodological issues in research with women]. In Ş. Yüksel, L. Gülseren, & A. D. Başterzi (Eds.). *Kadın Ruh Sağlığı.* (pp. 667-676). Türkiye Psikiyatri Derneği Yayınları.

Resnick, H. S., Kilpatrick D. G., Dansky B. S., Saunders B. E., & Best C. L. (1993). Prevalence of civilian trauma and posttraumatic stress disorder in a representative national sample of women. *Journal of Consulting and Clinical Psychology, 61*(6), 984-991.

Rogers, C. R. (1957). The necessary and sufficient conditions of therapeutic personality change. *Journal of Consulting Psychology,* 21, 95–103. http://dx.doi.org/10.1037/h0045357

Rose, J. (1985). Dora: Fragman and analysis. In C. Bernheimer, & C. Kahane (Eds.) *In Dora's Case: Freud-hysteria-feminism.* (pp. 128-148). New York: Columbia University Press.

Rush, F. (1977). Freud and the sexual abuse of children. *Chrysalis, 1*(1), 31-45.

Russell, D. E. H. (1984). *Sexual exploitation: Rape, child sexual abuse, and sexual harassment.* Beverly Hills: Sage.

Scully, D. (2013). *Understanding sexual violence: A study on convicted rapists.* Routledge.

Silverstein, L. B., & Goodrich, T. J. (Eds.). (2003). *Feminist family therapy: Empowerment in social context.* Washington, DC: American Psychological Association. http://dx.doi.org/10.1037/10615-000

Smith, A. J., & Siegel, R. F. (1985). Feminist therapy: Redefining power for the powerless. In L. B. Rosewater & L. E. A. Walker (Eds.), *Handbook of feminist therapy: Women's issues in psychotherapy* (pp. 13–21). New York, NY: Springer.
Stewart, D. E., & Robinson, G. E. (1998). A review of domestic violence and women's mental health. *Archives Women's Mental Health*, 1, 83–89.
Toronto, E., Ainslie, G., Donovan, M. W., Kelly, M., Kieffer, C., & McWilliams, N. (Eds.). (2005). Psychoanalytic reflections on a gender-free case: Into the void. New York, NY: Brunner-Routledge
Tsai, M., Gustafsson, T., Kanter, J., Plummer Louden, M., & Kohlenberg, R. (2017). Saying goodbyes to your clients: A functional analytic psychotherapy (FAP) perspective. *Psychotherapy: Theory, Research, Practice, 54*, 22–28.
Tummala-Narra, P. (2016). *Psychoanalytic theory and cultural competence in psychotherapy*. Washington, DC: American Psychological Association.
Walby, S. (1990). *Theorizing patriarchy*. Blackwell Publishers.
Walker, L. E. (1979). *The battered woman*. New York: Harper & Row.
Williams, E. F. (1995) *Voices of feminist therapy*, Harwood Academic Publishers.
Worell, J. & Remer, P. (2002). *Feminist perspectives in therapy: Empowering diverse women*, 2nd ed. Wiley.
Worell, J. (2000). Feminism: Feminist psychotherapy. In A. E. Kazdin (Ed.), *Encyclopedia of psychology* (Vol. 3, pp. 354–357). Oxford University Press.
Worell, J. E. & Johnson, N. G. (1997). *Shaping the future of feminist psychology: Education, research, and practice*. American Psychological Association.
Yüksel, Ş. (2012). Gündelik yaşamda şiddet, ruh sağlığı ve psikoterapi [Violence in everyday life, mental health and psychotherapy]. *Türkiye Psikiyatri Derneği Sürekli Eğitim/Sürekli Mesleki Gelişim Dergisi, 2*(3), 258-272.

A Feminist Voice in Mental Health from Turkey: Complicating Mainstream Knowledge and Practice

Şahika Yüksel

Emeritus Professor Istanbul University-Private Practice

The title of the article "A Feminist Voice in Mental Health from Turkey: Complicating Mainstream Knowledge and Practice" is overly ambitious. I have not conducted a feminist history study here. In the process of writing this article, I gathered information from various feminist friends. However, what I will be conveying here can only be the traces that remained with me. I would like to emphasize that, as with all complications on history that we ourselves have witnessed. "A Feminist Voice in Mental Health from Turkey: Complicating Mainstream Knowledge and Practice" reflects at most what the author remembers on the one hand and forgets on the other. In other words, I will convey my experiences as a feminist from Turkey.

I am a leftist woman who embraces the belief that every citizen is unconditionally entitled to human rights. As a physician and psychiatrist, I have been working for 50 years in an environment dominated by a traditional understanding of women's health. When I first started working in the field of mental health, I felt that the current practices were insufficient. Was it my own inability or inadequacy?

After completing my internship at Istanbul University's Istanbul Medical Faculty, Psychiatry Department, I received my first psychotherapy training in Cognitive Behavioral Therapy at the Institute of Psychiatry and the Group Analysis Institute in London. During my postgraduate education, I enhanced my skills as a psychotherapist, yet there was still much work to be done.

In this paper, I will also share examples of feminist activism from Turkey. Feminists have carried out numerous campaigns and demonstrations since the Yoğurtçu Park Women's March in 1987 up to the present day. They also published magazines and books. Following the 1980 coup in Turkey, my female colleagues from various disciplines and we began reading about feminism and participated in consciousness-raising groups. Through this process, we organized several public campaigns addressing violence against women, including violence by strangers in public spaces, domestic violence, and violence in detention centers. These initiatives received significant coverage in mainstream media and television.

For over 50 years, I have been seeing women who come to me with various problems and symptoms. However, general medical knowledge often fell short in explaining these issues and, most importantly, in helping them. During the first decade of my professional life, along with my feminist readings, I realized that gender discrimination and heterosexism profoundly affect all women's lives from childhood onward. I observed, with sadness and shame, how we normalize discrimination and violence in women's lives, viewing them as an inevitable fate.

It became clear that a different perspective was needed to alleviate women's pain, stop their tears, and prevent the recurrence of these issues. My medical practice also began to shift as I sought new methods and redefined my approach. In the early 1980s, after reading *Battered Wives* (Martin, 1976) - a gift from my feminist friend Gülnur Savran- I started cautiously asking women at the clinic about intimate partner violence.

However, in the beginning, I was not thinking about or questioning whether these women had been exposed to discrimination or violence. My mainstream medical and mental health education did not address the psychological effects of discrimination and violence. Once I realized the necessity of asking these questions, I learned how to approach them effectively. This marked my progress in therapy. Gender-based discrimination had not been taught to any of us. My clients were surprised but also relieved. They started sharing their experiences, describing the violence they endured at home, which was traditionally considered "normal" and "private." Initially, both my clients and I considered violence solely as physical harm. We did not give much importance to psychological violence, such as ignoring emotions, constant criticism, suppression of speech, and restriction of decision-making abilities.

Since becoming part of the feminist movement, my goals have evolved. During my second visit to London, I was there to learn something different. I attended workshops at the Women's Therapy Centre in London, which was pioneering feminist therapy with figures such as Susie Orbach (1983). Back in Istanbul, I began questioning clinical practices from a new perspective and considering the existence of discriminatory violence. I attended various human rights conferences. In 1992, at the World Trauma Congress, a "feminist therapists' dinner" was organized, where I met Judith Herman. She had written groundbreaking books on challenging topics, such as *Father-Daughter Incest* (Herman, 1993) and *Trauma and Recovery: The Aftermath of Violence - From Domestic Abuse to Political Terror* (Herman, 1992). I felt I had finally found the mentor I had been looking for. Those were the years when feminist research and work were just beginning to gain recognition in the Western world.

How was I to integrate what I had learned from the feminist movement into official mental health, that is, into clinical practice? I also brought these insights into professional training meetings. Many of my colleagues and students, most of whom were women, showed a growing interest in a feminist perspective. In the competitive world of academia, achieving rank was crucial for sharing and teaching what I had learned. In 1983, I became an associate professor, and by 1989, I had become a full professor in the psychiatry department of a medical faculty in Istanbul. It was no longer possible for the traditional, mainstream medical establishment to easily ignore me. So, I asked the following question: What can be done in light of everything I learned from feminists in Turkey and international feminist mental health workers? How could I bring my experiences to the professional organizations I was a part of, merge them with the experiences of my colleagues, and amplify our collective voice? (Yüksel, 2000; Yüksel et al., 2012; Yüksel et al., 2013).

The Turkish Medical Association (TMA), founded in 1953, has always been a progressive organization; however, sexism was not initially recognized as a critical issue by the association. The Psychiatric Association of Turkey (PAT) was established in 1996 by a group of young psychiatrists who had been working to create such an organization since the early 1990s. We started by forming a special working group focused on women's mental health. In larger groups and meetings, we began discussing the impact of sexual abuse on mental health. TMA eventually started organizing Women's Physicians and Women's Health meetings, although somewhat belatedly. The first congress was held in 2008.

I will discuss some of the challenges posed to the mainstream understanding by the TMA and the PAT, two professional organizations of which I am also a member. It is important to note that I am not the official voice of these organizations; these are my personal evaluations.

As mental health professionals, which steps do we have to follow in addressing sexism?

1. We should be aware of gender-based discrimination.
2. We should check every case and see if gender-based discrimination or violence is involved or not.
3. We should openly state gender-based discrimination or violence when we witness it.
4. When we witness gender-based discrimination or violence, we should implement scientific and ethical methods to empower the victim, punish the perpetrator, and ensure justice.

The first and second steps are our responsibility. If we cannot implement the third and fourth steps, we will have only detected the issue without taking any further action, thereby failing to ensure that justice is implemented. In medical practice, the principle of "do no harm" is paramount. However, professionals cannot always shield patients from harm entirely. The third and fourth steps of intervention can only be achieved in cases of violence. The expectations and circumstances of women subjected to violence vary widely. These differences are not solely personal but are also influenced by the social environment, family, and the larger community.

As therapists, we do not claim neutrality; we stand firmly against violence and discrimination. Our objective is to determine how we can collaboratively utilize our expertise with the individual to combat violence. We should employ all available methods without limiting ourselves to a single therapeutic approach. Numerous obstacles prevent women and LGBTQ+ individuals from disclosing the violence, especially sexual violence, they have faced. Ignoring these factors can lead to risks in interpreting experiences of violence.

We are acutely aware of the importance of collective activism. What are the needs of a woman receiving treatment at a health center who has endured physical or sexual violence? How urgent are these needs? Who is equipped to address these needs? What is her relationship with her non-offending relatives? Are they supportive? For her safety, with whom can we establish alliances? The answers to some of these questions may, in fact, imply crossing certain intimate boundaries within the therapeutic relationship with "women exposed to violence." Psychotherapy does not occur in isolation. We can explore these questions through various case examples. As professionals, how should we intervene in the cases we witness and where we gather evidence?

In the remaining portion, I would like to further explain my involvements through some examples.

1. KAMER (Women's Center) Southeastern Anatolian Studies
2. Against Sexual Harassment and Rape in Custody Project
3. Clinical and off-site women's groups: The example of Yezidi women
4. Turkish Medical Association Guidelines on the Prevention of Sexual Abuse and Promotion of Gender Equality.
5. Psychiatric Association of Turkey - Women's Mental Health Section: Guidelines for the Prevention of Sexual Abuse and Promotion of Gender Equality.

KAMER

It was founded in 1996 by a group of women in Diyarbakir who questioned violence against women both inside and outside the domestic space in 1994. The type of support offered by KAMER varies according to the situation. Today, there are 23 units operating in Diyarbakır and other locations in the region (KAMER, 1997).

Depending on the need, KAMER focuses on different areas. For example, 1138 asylum-seeking women who fled the war in Syria and settled in Diyarbakır, Gaziantep, Kilis, Mardin, and Şanlıurfa were interviewed in their respective cities of residence. After the February 2023 earthquake, psychosocial support in the native language was provided in the region. In the first six months,

1,250,993 earthquake survivors received humanitarian aid. Safe spaces were provided for refugee women and girls.

The KAMER Foundation has received numerous awards, including the Hrant Dink Award in 2019. In her study, Sezgin presents very promising outcomes based on her research conducted with women who have been exposed to trauma in either private or public spaces in the Southeastern Anatolian Region. Her study shows that only 60 hours of group psychotherapy applied to women who had been subjected to multiple traumas proved to be effective. This was no miracle; this study was carried out in collaboration with the KAMER (Sezgin & Punumaki, 2008).

Sexual Torture

The disclosure of sexual violence experienced by women is commonly experienced as a situation that could bring shame to the victim, rather than the perpetrator, and is more challenging than revealing other forms of violence, especially if the incident falls within the jurisdiction of the individual or organization responsible for the perpetration of sexual abuse. For this reason, I wanted to give separate attention to sexual abuse in custody.

Sexual torture represents a form of abuse that is particularly challenging to document. As time passes, sexual abuse and rape often leave few or no physical traces, although the psychological impact of these traumas tends to be long-lasting. Disclosure of sexual abuse remains difficult, regardless of the perpetrator's identity. Victims who confide in family members or therapists rarely pursue legal action, and even when they do, courts frequently dismiss cases due to 'insufficient evidence,' ensuring impunity for many offenders. Between 1997 and 2018, 101 women were reportedly raped in detention, while 498 others were subjected to sexual harassment (Bianet, 2018). Today, reports indicate that complaints of sexual abuse in prisons often go unanswered, and ill-treatment following such disclosures is not uncommon.

In response, a group of feminist lawyers established a project titled 'Against Sexual Harassment and Rape in Detention'. The lawyers involved in this project, including Eren Keskin, have referred clients who reported rape while in detention to our department at Istanbul University, Istanbul Medical Faculty, within the Psychiatry-Psychosocial Trauma Program.

Examinations of these cases were carried out at least one year after the assaults. Many victims were still detained at the time of evaluation and had only disclosed their experiences to their lawyers. Until their initial interactions with mental health professionals, they had not fully communicated their psychological and social challenges. For evaluations, we followed the 'Istanbul Protocol', a comprehensive clinical interview guideline that mandates medical reports and testimonies to be objective, relevant, and defensible in court. These reports include background information, findings, diagnostic tests, and assessments of the credibility of the testimonies. In contexts where torture and political violence are pervasive, evaluating the effects of such abuse requires a nuanced approach. According to Turkish law, privacy must be maintained during medical examinations of prisoners. However, guards are often required to stay in the examination room, compromising this privacy. Some women declined examinations under these conditions, while others consented to being examined in the presence of guards. We respected their decisions and adapted our methods to these limitations, prioritizing comfort and safety. If a prisoner needed and desired treatment, it was provided through our university's Psychosocial Trauma Program. Ensuring safety is the first step in trauma treatment, yet this is difficult to achieve in a prison environment where abusers retain authority. Our experiences treating individuals still in prison have been informative for our approach.

Despite the obstacles and adverse conditions faced during treatment, our efforts have positively contributed to the psychosocial functioning and wellbeing of the victims. It is imperative to break the silence surrounding violence. However, each disclosure must be addressed on an individual basis. Politically active women initially reported these abuses for political reasons, yet they later confronted the personal aspects of their trauma. One notable case is that of journalist Asiye Zeybek. Following our expert report, which was accepted as evidence, Zeybek appealed to the European Court of Human Rights (ECHR), which ruled in her favor. This resulted in Turkey paying a fine (Belge, 2001; Sezgin et al., 2000). Following this decision, those of us involved in writing the report faced various investigations, with accusations linking us to terrorist organizations.

While the "Against Sexual Harassment and Rape in Detention" project has been ongoing for 27 years, an Istanbul court has sentenced two police officers in the case concerning the strip search of two women during the 2013 Gezi Park protests (Bianet, 2024).

Yezidi Women

Every individual requires a safe home and family environment, free from abuse, to ensure comfort and provide support through daily life and during crises. The Yezidi population was forced to flee their homes due to occupation in 2014 (Shen, 2024). In response, the city of Diyarbakir provided shelter, initially accommodating approximately 4,000 Yezidis in camps. The Turkish Human Rights Foundation (TİHV) implemented a Psychosocial Support Program

(PSSP) to assist them, with around 600 individuals, predominantly women, seeking help (TİHV, 2017).

Direct communication with Yezidi women regarding their traumatic experiences was constrained. Information about their conditions was primarily obtained through male family members and community leaders, reflecting the prevailing patriarchal structure in which decisions concerning women's lives were predominantly made by men.

As the 'Right to the Highest Attainable Standard of Health' specifies, gender is not the only factor for conflict and violence in the family. Economic class and ethnic differentiation can also be important in relational hierarchies as well as structuring and shaping the family's mode of ruling. The additional factors, such as poverty, refugee status, and lack of education, are consistently linked to gender, contributing to the distinction between males and females in various situations (Cockburn, 1999).

These social norms and social barriers significantly influenced the therapeutic relationship with the victims. As mental health providers from a Muslim-majority country, we encountered unique challenges, particularly given that the Yezidis had suffered violence at the hands of individuals acting in the name of Islam. The Yezidi community, traditionally insular, delegates interactions with outsiders to men in higher echelons of their social hierarchy, complicating access to women's narratives. Consequently, obtaining direct information about women's personal and individual traumatic experiences was difficult. To date, no individual has disclosed experiences of sexual abuse or pregnancies resulting from rape. However, the absence of such admissions does not imply these events did not occur (Yüksel et al., 2018). Ten years after IS first launched its attack against the Yezidis, their suffering continues today, as thousands remain missing. Since 2014, Yezidi rights organizations and activists have been working with autonomous authorities to identify remaining Yezidis in detention in northeast Syria, coordinating between families and security forces (Amnesty International, 2024).

Turkish Medical Association Guidelines on the Prevention of Sexual Abuse and Promotion of Gender Equality

The work of the Women Physicians and Women's Health Section of the Istanbul Chamber of Physicians, which started in 2014, was endorsed at the 73rd Grand Congress of the TMA. The aim is to prevent discrimination by physicians against colleagues or third parties on the grounds of sex, sexual orientation, gender identity, or any other criteria; to prevent sexual violence and all forms of violence against women; and to combat gender inequality as a source of such discrimination. This directive covers sexual violence, abuse, and all forms of violence against women, including third parties, women, LGBTI+s, and children, where at least one of the parties involved is a physician (TMA, 2021).

Sexual abuse is difficult to disclose, and it is necessary to conduct private sessions sensitively. Complaints on this issue are handled by a special committee of the relevant chamber of physicians. Units have already been established in nine cities (TMA, 2021).

The Psychiatric Association of Turkey – Women and Mental Health Section (PAT-WMHS)

It prepared a political guideline on gender, gender discrimination, and sexual abuse in 2021 (PAT, 2021). This guideline establishes an effective, reliable, and confidential application mechanism that considers the testimony of the applicant fundamental in addressing all forms of discrimination and sexual abuse against women and LGBTI+ individuals. The document addresses forms of harassment that contribute to a hostile work environment, as well as harassment involving incentives, misuse of authority, and tactics aimed at coercing consent, including threats of abandonment for noncompliance.

The growing efforts of feminist mental health professionals in Turkey are not only aimed at supporting individuals in their psychological recovery but also at fostering a profound social transformation. These professionals approach gender-based violence not merely as an individual trauma but as a societal issue, shaping their work accordingly. In 2013, we published the book titled *Women's Lives and Women's Mental Health*, by PAT Publications under the Women and Mental Health Section. We knew that in therapeutic sessions with women who have experienced intimate partner violence or sexual assault, they emphasize the underlying gender norms and patriarchal structures that contribute to these traumas. This approach not only empowers victims with individual resilience but also helps them gain awareness of systemic injustices, enabling them to find their voices.

The work of feminist mental health professionals also supports calls for legal and institutional changes to prevent violence against women in Turkey. Many feminist therapists and psychiatrists participate in or lead various social support programs and public education projects aimed at preventing gender-based violence. These professionals collaborate with non-governmental organizations and women's shelters such as Mor Çatı (Purple Roof) to ensure that victims have access to safe spaces and resources. Additionally, the increasing presence of feminist-oriented mental health practitioners is creating a shift in educational frameworks, promoting gender awareness among future mental health professionals. This feminist approach represents a crucial step toward supporting both individual healing and societal change in Turkey.

Effective Interventions for Survivors of Violence

How can women exposed to violence regain their power and autonomy? Effective interventions for survivors of violence require a multi-level approach, encompassing individual, community-based, and global efforts to address the complexities of their experiences.

Individual Level

Psychotherapy and counseling are essential in helping survivors process trauma and develop coping mechanisms. Therapeutic interventions aim to restore a sense of agency and resilience in survivors, helping them navigate both immediate and long-term psychological challenges at an individual level.

Psychotherapy for Survivors of Violence

Psychotherapy for survivors of violence against women is essential, but it must be adapted to the unique context of each survivor. Although the techniques may be similar to those used with other clients, therapy for survivors requires heightened sensitivity to issues of power dynamics and safety. The settings for mental health services vary widely, from hospital emergency clinics to women's shelters. In many cases, women may seek help not only in healthcare facilities but also in courthouses or community organizations. It is crucial to address family dynamics and the damaging effects of violence, defining boundaries, setting realistic goals, and encouraging decision-making skills within the therapeutic process.

Effective therapy does not solely focus on individual healing but also involves addressing broader social values. Women may initially describe their issues as "communication problems" to conceal the underlying domestic violence. Therapists need to create a safe space for survivors to gradually reveal the full extent of their experiences and challenges (PAT, 2024).

Community Level

Community-based interventions play a critical role in providing support outside of formal therapeutic settings. Non-governmental organizations (NGOs), social support networks, public education initiatives, and programs that promote anti-sexism and anti-violence are integral to creating a supportive environment for survivors. These community resources can offer safe spaces, emotional support, and practical assistance, which are often inaccessible within traditional family structures, especially in societies where family honor and privacy are prioritized over individual well-being.

The Role of Social Support Networks

Psychotherapy alone is insufficient to drive broad social change; an effective social support network is essential in a survivor's life. In traditional societies, family ties are significant, but they may also impose secrecy and shame around violence within the family. The Turkish proverb, "the arm breaks but stays within the sleeve," exemplifies this cultural tendency to conceal family issues. Our work has shown that survivors often receive limited support from their original family structures. As a result, alternative support systems and safe shelters are crucial. Public institutions dedicated to addressing domestic violence must collaborate to establish and maintain these resources. The World Health Organization (WHO) suggests that there should be one shelter available for every 10,000 inhabitants to adequately support survivors.

Global Level

Legislative frameworks and international conventions are necessary to establish and enforce the rights of survivors. Global conventions, such as those advocated by the United Nations or WHO, provide guidelines for countries to implement policies that protect individuals from gender-based violence. However, the effectiveness of these policies depends on their consistent application and enforcement.

The Psychotherapeutic Relationship and the Process of Change

The psychotherapeutic relationship is inherently complex, requiring a collaborative effort between the client and therapist to understand and systematically address the survivor's problems. Therapy involves not only discussion but also active engagement in strategies that facilitate change. Therapists are responsible for maintaining up-to-date knowledge and delivering competent interventions that adhere to the ethical principle of "do no harm."

Choosing the Appropriate Therapy Format

The format of therapy can vary, including individual, group, or couples sessions. Group therapy, particularly with other survivors of domestic violence, can be instrumental in reducing the sense of isolation that many survivors experience. Group sessions provide a space where survivors can share their stories, recognize commonalities, and build solidarity, which contributes to the healing process (Sezgin & Punamaki, 2008; Yüksel et al. 1999).

Effective support for survivors of violence requires a coordinated, multifaceted approach that spans individual therapeutic interventions, community support structures, and legislative actions on a global scale. Each level of intervention plays a crucial role in empowering survivors and fostering resilience in the face of violence and trauma.

Recognition of Violence against Women as a Human Rights Issue

Recognizing violence against women as a fundamental human rights violation has been essential in shifting the perception of such violence from a private, family matter to a public issue requiring government intervention. This acknowledgment underscores the responsibility of authorities to protect women's rights and ensure justice for victims, contributing to a societal change in how violence against women is addressed.

Economic and Educational Empowerment

Providing women with economic and educational opportunities is critical in reducing their dependence on family members or others who may perpetrate violence against them and their children. Economic independence enables women to make safer choices, seek support, and leave abusive situations if necessary. Educational programs also equip women with knowledge about their rights and available resources, enhancing their ability to seek assistance.

Culturally and Ethnically Sensitive Interventions

Effective interventions must consider cultural and ethnic diversity to address the unique needs of victims and family members. Tailoring interventions to align with cultural contexts increases their accessibility and effectiveness, making it more likely that individuals from diverse backgrounds will seek and benefit from these services.

Affordable and Culturally Sensitive Preventive Measures

Developing low-cost, culturally sensitive preventive programs is crucial for reaching a larger group of victims. These measures should be accessible to large groups, raising awareness about violence prevention and offering support to at-risk individuals. Community outreach, public education campaigns, and workshops in schools and workplaces can serve as preventive strategies, fostering a culture of zero tolerance for violence (UN Women 2019, UN Women 2023, UN Women 2024).

Progress over the Last 30 Years in Turkey

Significant progress has been made in Turkey over the past three decades in addressing violence against women. Although it is now widely recognized that sexual assault occurs and is a pervasive issue in society, there remain gaps in delivering adequate justice. The number of trained medical and legal professionals involved in supporting survivors and prosecuting offenders has increased. Additionally, there has been growth in education and training programs related to violence against women. However, the expansion of these initiatives is still insufficient to meet the high demand, underscoring the need for continued efforts in professional training and public awareness.

Last words - what we learned: Moving from being a "Bystander" to being an "Upstander".

Acknowledgements

Special thanks for their comment to my dear feminist friends Suzan Saner, Gülnur Savran, and Ayşe Devrim Başterzi.

References

Amnesty International (2024, July 31) *Syria: Yezidi survivors of Islamic State atrocities abandoned to indefinite detention in north-east Syria.* Retrieved from https://www.amnesty.org/en/latest/news/2024/07/syria-yezidi-survivors-of-islamic-state-atrocities-abandoned-to-indefinite-detention-in-north-east-syria/

Bianet. (2018, November 26). Son 21 yılda 601 kadın gözaltında cinsel tacize ve tecavüze uğradı [601 Women subjected to sexual harassment, rape in detention in Last 21 Years]. https://bianet.org/haber/son-21-yilda-601-kadin-gozaltinda-cinsel-tacize-ve-tecavuze-ugradi-202947

Bianet (2024, October 17). Gezi'de çıplak arama davası: Mücella Yapıcı'nın şikayetçi olduğu iki polise hapis cezası [Two police officers sentenced for strip search during 2013 Gezi Park protests]. Bianet. https://bianet.org/haber/gezide-ciplak-arama-davasi-mucella-yapicinin-sikayetci-oldugu-iki-polise-hapis-cezasi-300833

Belge, B. (2001, August 21) Asiye Zeybek Güzel ve öyküsü [Asiye Zeybek Güzel and her story]. https://bianet.org/haber/asiye-zeybek-guzel-ve-oykusu-4812

Cockburn, C. (1999). *Buradan baktığımızda kadınların militarizme karşı mücadelesi [When we look at it from here, women's struggle against militarism].* Metis Yayınları.

Herman, J. L. (1992). *Trauma and recovery: The aftermath of violence - From domestic abuse to political terror.* New York: Basic Books.

Herman, J. L. (1993). Father—daughter incest. In *International handbook of traumatic stress syndromes* (pp. 593-600). Boston, MA: Springer US.

KAMER Foundation (1997). *About us.* Retrieved from https://www.kamer.org.tr/eng/icerik_detay.php?id=270

Martin, D (1976) *Battered wives.* Pocket Book.

Orbach, S. (1983). *What do women want?* Penguin Michael Joseph.

Sezgin, A. U., Yüksel, Ş., & Keser, V. (2000). Gözaltında tecavüz ve cinsel saldırılarda raporun yeri. *Türkiye insan hakları vakfı tedavi ve rehabilitasyon merkezleri raporu,* (pp. 51-63) TİHV Yayınları, Ankara. https://tihv.org.tr/wp-content/uploads/2020/03/2000-Tedavi-ve-Rehabilitasyon-Merkezleri-Raporu.pdf

Sezgin, U., & Punamaki, R. L. (2008) Effectiveness of group psychotherapy among women with multiple traumatic life events: A pilot study in the southeast Anatolian region. *Journal of Loss & Trauma, 13*(6), 557-575.

Shen, A. (2024). *Soykırımın 10. yılında Ezidi kadınlar*. Çatlak Zemin. Retrieved from https://catlakzemin.com/soykirimin-10-yilinda-ezidi-kadinlar/

The Psychiatric Association of Turkey/PAT (2021). Cinsiyet ayrımcılığı, cinsel şiddet ve tacize karşı politika belgesi [Policy document against gender discrimination, sexual violence and harassment]. https://psikiyatri.org.tr/TPDData/Uploads/files/cinselsiddettutumbelgesi-21052021.pdf

The Psychiatric Association of Turkey/PAT (2024) Kadına yönelik şiddette psikolojik ilk yardım (LIVES)[Psychological first aid in violence against women (LIVES)] Çevrimiçi Yayın. https://tpdyayin.psikiyatri.org.tr/BookShopData/LIVES2024.pdf

The Turkish Medical Association/TMA (2021, July 2). Cinsel şiddeti önleme ve toplumsal cinsiyet eşitliğini destekleme yönergesi [Directive on preventing sexual violence and promoting gender equality]. https://www.ttb.org.tr/mevzuat_goster.php?Guid=bbafc53c-63c8-11ec-87e9-2806a62df02b

The Turkish Human Rights Foundation/TİHV (2017). *2016-2017 Study report*, p.43-44. https://tihv.org.tr/wp-content/uploads/2020/03/2017-%C3%87al%C4%B1%C5%9Fma-Raporu.pdf

UN Women (2019). *RESPECT Women: Preventing violence against women*. United Nations Entity for Gender Equality and the Empowerment of Women and World Health Organization. Retrieved from https://www.unwomen.org/en/digital-library/publications/2019/05/respect-women-preventing-violence-against-women

UN Women (2024) *Women's economic empowerment strategy*. United Nations Entity for Gender Equality and the Empowerment of Women. Retrieved from https://www.unwomen.org

UN Women (2023) *Focusing on prevention: Ending violence against women*. United Nations Entity for Gender Equality and the Empowerment of Women. Retrieved from https://www.unwomen.org

Yüksel, Ş., Kora, K., Enderer, M., Karali, N., Gök Ş., & Tunalı, D. (1999). Group treatment for domestic violence in Turkish women. *The Behaviour Therapist, 22*, 1667-173.

Yüksel, Ş. (2000) Collusion and denial of childhood sexual trauma in traditional societies. In A. Y. Schalev, R. Yehuda, A. C. McFarlane (Eds.), *International handbook of human response to trauma*. The Plenum Publisher, 153-163.

Yüksel, Ş., Cindoğlu, D., & Sezgin, U. (2012). Women's bodies, sexualities and human rights. In M. Dudley, D. Silove, F. Gale (Eds.), *Mental health and human rights*. Oxford University Press, 440-447.

Yüksel, Ş., Gülseren, L., & Başterzi, A. D. (2013). Kadınların yaşamı ve kadın ruh sağlığı (Women's life and mental health) TPD 16, Ankara.

Yüksel, Ş. Saner, S., Başterzi, A. D., Oglagu, Z, & Bülbül, İ. (2018). Genocidal sexual assault on women and the role of culture in the rehabilitation process: Experiences from working with Yazidi women in Turkey. International Rehabilitation Council for Torture Victims. *Torture Journal, 28*(3), 123-132.

From Feminist Clinics to Women's Healing Circles: Women's Reproductive and Holistic Health from the 70s to Today

Ayşe Dayı

Founder and Director, Orca Dreams Platform for Mindful Living

Reconnecting to Our Sacred Feminine and Exploring Identity and Our Deepest Desires

It has been 2 years now that I have been facilitating women's circles in Berlin, where I have been living since 2018. The circles are called "Remembering & Honoring my Sacred Feminine: A Women's Healing Circle on Gender, Body & Sexuality."

I started these circles (in English and Turkish) with the heartfelt intention of honoring the feminine, reconnecting to our wild and sacred sides, and feeling our authentic and delicious power.

In these circles, in each session we take up a theme (i.e., Gender, Reconnecting to our Wild Feminine, Sexualization of the Body, Menstruation, Childbirth, Motherhood, and Connecting to Mother Earth). In the session on the Wild Feminine, I guide a meditation in which we see ourselves approaching and joining a large circle of women sitting on a brightly lit full moon night. Our mothers and foremothers are also in the circle. When the time comes, each woman rises and sings a song. The quest is: sing us (an answer to) "who are you?" and "what are your deepest desires?" When your time comes, you rise and sing a beautiful song, one that you have never heard before, with sounds and melodies coming out of your throat and mouth that surprise you. After all the women sing their song, the group falls silent all at once. The fire in the middle of the circle starts fading, and the moon gives way to dawn... All rise in harmony, smile at each other, and get ready to meet the new day.

This chapter is a journey of women's sexual and reproductive health care from the 1970s to today, through what I learned and distilled in my research, activism, and recent work on the intersections of mindfulness, consciousness, and feminine rising. In short, we will explore together here herstory of reproductive care from the 1970s Women's Health Movement and its offshoots of Feminist Clinics to today's women's circles.

As in the song of the women's circle that asked us who we are and what we deeply desire, while reading this chapter, I invite us to hold in our minds and hearts the following three questions:

- What are women's deepest desires in terms of women's health care, reproductive health care, and healing? (Women, meaning cis- and transwomen)
- What are the alternative (dignified) models for reproductive care?
- What may women's reproductive health and healing look like? (What can we learn from the past, and how can we reimagine and reconstruct the present and the future?)

Learnings on Women's Reproductive Health Care and Rights

In the years 2001-2002, for my Ph.D., I researched the legacy of the Women's Health Movement (WHM) in the U.S., through an ethnographic study of two Women's Health Centers, especially on the aims of the movement to empower women in reproductive care and to transform medical education and practice towards a less medicalized, more dignified reproductive care for women.

Dating back to the 1830s and 1840s (Zimmermann & Hill, 2000), the U.S. Women's Health Movement (WHM) peaked in the late 1960s and early 1970s in the U.S., this time as a grassroots movement with an extensive critique of women's healthcare in the areas of doctor-patient relationships, contraceptive safety and access, abortion rights, sterilization abuses, medicalization of childbirth, and excessive and unnecessary use of gynecological and breast surgery (Morgen, 2002). This critique was historically contextualized within the establishment of Western medicine and the systematic exclusion of females from medicine and gynecology and the subsequent medicalization of normal female reproductive events (e.g. birth control, birth, abortion, menstruation, and menopause) under the biomedical model of Western medicine which pathologized the event (e.g. PMS and menopause treatments), put women in the role of a "patient" who is passive and without much knowledge on her body, and justified the use of unnecessary medical and technological practices and interventions. A beautiful example of this that I have used in my teaching and now in women's circles comes from the medicalization of childbirth, where the lying down position in birth was only invented for the convenience of the (male) ob/gyn, whereas women have and still use standing, squatting, half sitting (on midwifery stools), and many other positions to use the force of gravity for better pushing and giving birth, utilizing the wisdom of their bodies.

Women's Reproductive and Holistic Health from the 70s to Today   63

As I will discuss in the later sections of this paper, to this initial critique of WHM, intersections of racism and sexism and technology and medicine and capitalism were added by feminist scholars and activists. WHM advocates worked for:

- Increased control for women in the decisions and actions impacting their bodies and health
- Affordable and accessible reproductive care (in birth control, abortion, birth and all)
- Demedicalization of women's reproductive life events and problems
- Information on women's health issues, more emphasis on prevention and less use of invasive treatments
- A relationship of respect and dignity between the provider and women (with sensitivity to gender, race, class, sexuality)
- Adoption of a socio-medical (vs. a biomedical) model of health
- Increase in women in medicine (as physicians and paraprofessionals)
- Increase in women's health research
- A commitment to healthcare as a right, protected by legislative measures that protect reproductive rights and access to care regardless of financial and insurance status. (Dayi, 2009; Morgen, 2002)

Fascinated by this movement and its very detailed and wise critique of (women's) health, I was curious to find out its legacy in the 2000s, namely 30 years after its peak in the 1960s and 1970s. Specifically, I wanted to explore how women who received reproductive (especially birth control and abortion) care and the staff who provided these services, understood and experienced *reproductive empowerment*. I was also curious about whether and how medical education and practice had been transformed, as well as what demedicalized care looked (and felt) like in action. I discuss the findings of this research in detail in previous articles on empowerment (Dayi, 2009) and organizational strategies, specifically how the Women's Health Centers negotiated and maneuvered the increasingly capitalist technobiomedicine and the New Right and anti-abortion forces (Dayi, 2011). In this chapter, I would like to zoom in on findings on the concept of empowerment and the nonmedical feminist model of care.

What I did was to visit (during 2001 and 2002) two women's health centers (one of which continued as a feminist collective) in the Northeast region of the U.S. for two weeks at each site. At the sites, I conducted semi-structured interviews with staff and women, did observations, took field notes, and completed reviews of agency materials (e.g., forms, newsletters, etc.). Both centers were established by women, in the years (in 1974 and 1978) following the Roe v. Wade decision to legalize abortion in the U.S., with the aim of providing low-cost abortion in their respective communities. Both centers were women-controlled settings, where women occupied key positions and ran the clinic. The doctors who provided the abortions were contracted personnel and were not included on the board. Both centers provided medical and surgical abortions, expanded gyn care, including routine gyn exams, colposcopy, STI (Sexually Transmitted Infections) checks, birth control counseling, provision and renewal. I conducted (a) interviews with staff (n=21) (b) interviews with women receiving care (n=24), (c) observations of pre-abortion counseling sessions and gyn visits (n=16), (d) took field notes on staff-staff, staff-client interactions, protesters, spatial arrangement of the centers, and conversations with staff, (e) review of agency forms and archival materials. I used a poststructural feminist framework and a Grounded Theory Approach to analyze the data.

Empowerment as Safety and Dignity

The WHM advocates had demanded, and through these centers, still worked on the empowerment of women in reproductive care, which meant women having increased control (over information and action). The results of this research revealed that empowerment (specifically in the areas of birth control and abortion) was experienced not as taking control, but rather as safety and humane care. Safety had two dimensions: meaning both physical and emotional safety, and humane treatment meant dignified, egalitarian, individualized, and holistic care.

Physical safety meant both being protected from anti-abortion providers (being in a safe environment) and receiving a safe abortion care. One overall finding of the research was that the WHM was successful in bringing women physicians back to medicine (after the historical exclusion of midwives and women healers from medical education and practice), and increasing research on women's health, adoption of informed consent and information on side effects of contraceptives, etc., and a bit of training of ob/gyn students on how to do gyn exams in a respectful way (e.g., informing the woman of the steps, seeing the woman first clothed etc.). These were successful changes of medical education and practice. However, the movement could not fully transform the medical establishment in reproductive health. In addition, when the Women's Health Centers were established as autonomous entities, outside of the mainstream medical/health practice, in the context of the U.S., with its increasing antiabortion movement, it made these centers easy targets for protesters and radical groups.

Both centers in my research had direct contact with Operation Rescue, an extremist antiabortion organization that conducts blockades, occupations, sit ins, etc. They further experienced arson attacks, stink bomb attacks, vigils, and protests. As a result, they applied measures of high security like cameras, IDs, and locked entrances to the surgery and aftercare rooms. For the women receiving care, coming to a place where they would be safe from protesters (and in a respectful environment) was important.

Physical safety also meant receiving care in a safe way. The centers addressed the risks of possible complications of abortion by providing information in pre-abortion counseling sessions, as well as holding a 24-hour hotline for emergencies and a required follow-up exam.

Emotional safety had dimensions such as receiving care in a comfortable, homey atmosphere, as well as receiving non-judgmental and non-directive care. To me, this dimension, along with the dignified care, are important dimensions of the alternative models of care for women.

In both centers, the waiting rooms, counseling, exam, and operation rooms, were arranged in a non-medical way. Instead of white walls, sterile surfaces, and white aprons, etc., the space was decorated in a homey way, pastel colors, pictures on the walls, mellow lighting, a TV or music in the waiting room and exam rooms, and little touches like tea and crackers in the after-care area, little hearts on the walls of the waiting room and exam rooms with empowering messages from women who had previously received care from the agency, nice *cloth* gowns for gyn exams and abortion (instead of paper gowns), socks placed on the gyn exam forks, and lavender sachets in the room. For most women, for whom the gynecological exams and abortion create anxiety and vulnerability, this atmosphere, coupled with friendly and welcoming staff who treated them in a more peer-like manner, comforted women and provided them with a vision of how women's care can be.

Receiving care in a way that is not judgmental of their sexuality, or decisions, was also an important part of emotional safety, thus felt empowering for women. Many women, including young, non-heterosexual, unmarried women, feel judged for their sexuality in mainstream gynecology practice, as we also found in our study on Turkish health restructuring (Dayi & Karakaya, 2018). Non-directive care meant receiving all information on birth control and abortion possibilities and being allowed to make one's own decision without being cajoled into a choice. I remember the "director" of the Feminist Health Center telling me that women were told that their decision is fully respected, and they can change their decision on abortion on the table.

Humane care meant receiving dignified, egalitarian, individualized, and holistic care. Receiving *dignified care* included receiving all information that is provided in an interactive and non-medical/non-technical way, and not being rushed (having time for questions, concerns, less waiting time, and returning of their calls to the center). Dignified care also meant *not feeling as a number*. Being treated as a number in mainstream care was closely linked to degradation, punishment, demeaning, and dehumanization. Measures such as talking with women fully clothed first (before a gyn exam), homey atmosphere, chit chat staff had with women, taking care not to show bloody instruments made women feel respected and treated individually and not as a number in an assembly line.

Egalitarian care meant being treated as a peer. Even though women did not express a desire to be equal with the providers, they did notice and appreciate the friendly, peer-like approach of the staff, and the encouragement to call the staff (including the doctors) by their first names. *Individualized care* meant that the service accommodated the different individual needs, knowledge, and wisdom of the women, as well as their individual reactions to abortion and birth control. Individualized care also meant privacy, receiving services in private and not feeling "herded." *Holistic care* meant being recognized and treated as a whole person. This was done in the centers by providing information (e.g. pamphlets) on women's wellbeing in general (e.g. violence against women) and providing non-reproductive services like counseling and massage, and the provider's emphasis on women's overall health.

This research revealed the intricate intersectional workings of medicine, state, and the new Right (anti-abortion movement in the U.S.). Women's empowerment in reproductive care and rights and the work of the Feminist Clinics I visited, were embedded in and depended on medicine (the level of medicalization of reproductive care), state laws and regulations on abortion which were getting direr each year, and the rise of the New Right and antiabortion movement.

Reproductive Technologies and Women's Bodies

I would now like to add to the knowledge above on how reproductive technologies (in interaction with the factors listed above: medicine, state, and the New Right) affect women's reproductive care and rights and redefine pregnancy and motherhood. In my article entitled "A Feminist Ethics Approach to Sexuality and Reproduction: Fetal Personhood and Women's Bodily Integrity" (Dayi, 2017), I tracked the technological creation and historical/cultural production of the modern fetus through imaging technologies, starting from Samuel Thomas Soemmering's anatomical drawings of fetuses (in 1799), who were drawn without connection to the uterus or the woman (Duden, 1999), to electrophotography (the famous image of Lennart Nilsson in Life magazine in 1965, of the fetus that floats independently in space and the womb and women disappear into Space) and reproductive technologies such as ultrasound, surrogacy, and fetal surgery. Without going into much detail here, I would like to emphasize how such technologies divided the pregnant woman into woman and fetus, who are juxtaposed against each other, aided the technofetus to gain personhood (in legal and biomedical discourse and practices) while the women, whose bodily integrity was violated (her body borders becoming more and more permeable), started disappearing into empty space or became a "womb environment" or "incubator" for the "unborn child." I end the article with a feminist ethics approach to this transformation. An important detail here is that, how, for example, in ultrasound in prenatal exams, continuous fetal monitoring used in childbirth, and in fetal surgery, women start experiencing their pregnancy through technology and the machine, losing contact and trust in the wisdom of their bodies. Women undergoing prenatal ultrasounds and who feel fetal movement may be told by technicians that they should not be feeling any fetal movement at the pregnancy stage in which they are (and thus to trust the technology over their own bodily experience), or women who receive epidural and lose their ability to feel the contractions and the ability to push, may follow their contractions on the screen of the fetal monitor. Another significant point is on the redefining of pregnancy and motherhood through surrogacy, where women "rent" their wombs and carry a pregnancy for commercial reasons, where the class and race inequalities play major roles in the treatment of the surrogate women/mothers. I also discussed, how in the context of the U.S. anti-abortion movement and legislations that interact with medicine, pregnant women are criminalized (face arrests or forced C-Sections) for harming their fetus (which is treated in law as an "unborn person" already).

All of these consequences of reproductive technologies alert us to the dimension of dignity in reproductive care and rights: the need to honor and protect women's bodily integrity (which is protected in human and medical / patient rights), and in the creation and adoption of technologies, taking care not to reproduce the view of women's bodies as machines (which is also reproduced in medicalized births where the birth is treated as an assembly-line procedure), and pregnancy and birth are seen as technical and (in surrogacy) contractual issues where women disassociate from their bodies. In Casper's (1998) book on fetal surgery, there is a very telling quote of a pregnant woman, who says she was so focused on the surgery that she forgot that the operation on the fetus was going to be through her, she was the one who was undergoing this serious surgery with high risks to her and the fetus.

Before going on, I would also like to add the dimension of race and racism here. Roberts (1998) reminds us how for non-white, and especially Black women, surrogacy reminds them of slavery, where the slave woman bore children over which she had no rights. Roberts also discusses the intersections of racism and classism limiting the rights of the surrogate mother. Kapsalis (2002) also discussed the racist and sexist history of the speculum used in gynecological exams today, explaining how this tool was initially tested on slave women with pain, violating again bodily integration and the Hippocratic oath of not causing harm. All of this reminds us that technologies, and reproductive technologies, are never neutral but their creation and use depend on the social context, cultural, and historical in/equalities. Perhaps then, in the new era, we may prioritize and create reproductive technologies that honor and increase women's dignity, and celebrate pregnancy and childbirth, instead of demeaning and traumatizing women.

Reproductive Care and Rights in the Context of Neoliberal Health Reforms

The last body of research and activism I will discuss here come from my latest research on the effect of neoliberal health restructuring on women's reproductive care and rights. With my colleague and friend Eylem Karakaya, we investigated how the neoliberal health restructuring in Turkey affected reproductive care and rights in Turkey, in the areas of birth control, abortion, gynecological care, and childbirth. Because the neoliberal restructuring of health involved the restructuring of the Family Health Centers (FHC), the places where many women receive their basic birth control methods, gyn care, and contraceptive counselling for free, we took them as our main sites.

Between 2014 and 2015, we collected data from Family Health Center (FHC) workers (physicians, nurses, and nurse-midwives), and from women receiving reproductive care from these centers, other public centers, private gynecologists, and from public and private hospitals in five cities: İstanbul, İzmir, Van, Diyarbakır, and Gaziantep. We completed surveys with women (aged 18–45) in four of these cities (n=313); surveys in Diyarbakir and Antep with reproductive health personnel who worked in the public sector at the primary and secondary levels (n=103); and focus groups with women aged 18–45 (n=19), and focus groups (n=9) and individual interviews (n=3) with FHC personnel in all cities except Van. The personnel interviewed were from 12 FHCs and from one AÇSAP centre. All interviews were transcribed verbatim and analysed using a grounded theory approach.

We found out how the neoliberal mechanisms (such as restructuring of Family Health Centers and hospitals with mechanisms of privatization, bureaucratization, implantation of performance points for doctors, nurses and midwives) were applied together with a growing neo-conservative discourse and implementations on abortion, childbirth / C-sections and pronatalist (anti-abortion) population planning discourse and measures of the government, led to (1) the indebtedness of women through out-of-pocket payments for private contraceptive and abortion care; (2) the indebtedness of physicians, nurses, and midwives to the state through salary cuts from missed performance targets (and the use of fraud to avoid missed targets); (3) a reduction in the quality of existing reproductive care (such as prenatal follow-ups); and (4) a reduction in access to reproductive care itself (namely decreases in contraception, sexual / reproductive counselling, and in abortion). We discussed these in detail in Dayı

Women's Reproductive and Holistic Health from the 70s to Today 69

and Karakaya (2018) and in Dayı (2019). In Dayı (2019), I discussed how neoliberal mechanisms used in tandem with conservative discourse did in Turkey (as they did in the U.S.) lead to the erosion of the right to abortion and contraception without changing the abortion law or official policies on contraception themselves.

In our chapter in the edited book *The Politics of the Female Body in Contemporary Turkey: Reproduction, Maternity and Sexuality* (Alkan et al., 2021), Eylem Karakaya and I discussed another interesting part of this research. Using women's narratives, we investigated sexual and reproductive rights violations in contemporary Turkey, in the areas of abortion, birth control, birth, and routine gynecological care. We specifically focused on: (a) the continuities in rights violations (prior to health restructuring), (b) the exasperation of certain rights violations that accompanied this neoliberal health restructuring that is coupled with conservative discourse and policies (including the new pro-natalist policy), and (c) the new rights violations that came into being because of neoliberal policies and conservative pressure (Dayı & Karakaya, 2021).

It was here that my research and activism had come full circle, where women in the U.S. (who received care from Feminist Health Centers) and women in Turkey receiving care from public and private sectors were connected in their understanding of, and desires for, safe and dignified care. The Turkish women mentioned a desire for *non-judgmental care*, where they were properly informed about the care *(informed consent and care)*, the *right to privacy*, the basic right of *being free from gynecological violence* in all areas of care (gynecological exam, contraception counseling and provision, abortion care and childbirth), and *the right to accessible contraception and abortion for all women.*

In our book chapter, we discuss in detail which of these right violations continued through the neoliberal health restructuring, which deepened, or were added as new violations because of neoliberal and neoconservative measures. We highlight how, many -if not all- of these rights, already come under (and thus in theory should be protected) by patient rights in Turkey as well as the international agreements (e.g., CEDAW, ICPD, U.N.'s SDGs) to which Turkey is a signatory. We, however, alert to how the global neoliberal context is shrinking the applicability and enforcement of these agreements through excluding feminist organizations and individuals from decision making both within countries and in global meetings.

Remembering and Honoring Our Sacred Feminine: Women's Healing Circles

As I mentioned at the beginning, currently I work with women in a non-academic, more holistic context, combining the academic and activist knowledge and wisdom (including the ones mentioned up to here), with mindfulness and embodied approaches that include meditation, art (writing, painting, dancing), qigong, reading, watching documentaries, visiting exhibits and sharing in the circle format.

I have been holding women's circles at the VHS: Volkshochschule, Mitte in Berlin in English for the last 3 years and had the same circle in Turkish for a shorter period at a Family Center in Berlin as well. The aim of these circles is to join the global wave of the rise of the feminine and the Sacred Feminine that is seen and felt across the globe (as seen, for example, in the rise of female leadership from Greta to Latin American leaders and the 13 Grandmothers) and explore our femininity collectively in a circle, in order to liberate our minds and bodies of cultural notions of shame, guilt, imperfection, and limited expression in the world, to discover and reconnect to our Sacred Femininity, to the ancient wisdom of our bodies and sexuality, and create new ways of being that are more healing, balanced, and whole. We use meditation, movement, artwork, writing, films, reading and of course sharing of experience, not intellectually or theoretically, but from experience and from the heart. Each session has a theme: Gender, Wild and Sacred Feminine, Sexualization of the Body, Childbirth & Birthing the New, Life Cycles of a Woman & Menstruation, Motherhood, and Relationship to Mother Earth. Sometimes some sessions are facilitated or co-facilitated by other participants who volunteer to do so. Participants have been diverse: Turkish, German, American, Dutch, French, Egyptian, single or partnered, with and without children, heterosexual and lesbian. As for readings, I use the writings of Fatima Mernissi, Clarissa Pinkola Estes, Emily Martin, as well as readings on the history of childbirth and on capitalist and medical impact on menstruation and more.

What attracts women to the circle is their experience of the oppression and degradation, as well as their sensing the current Rise of the Feminine, their desire to heal the wounds, the longing for sisterhood (to be with other women in a safe, joyful, nourishing space), and the wish to discover their own femininity and balance their feminine and masculine sides. Many women felt that they had suppressed their femininity, becoming overly masculine, and now wanted to rediscover their gender and sexuality with other women. Our sessions are always very sincere, where each of us listens to the one speaking and contributes to collective wisdom by sharing her story and perspective. The sisterhood created in the circle makes it safe and joyful for women to be able to freely express themselves and to re-discover their own femininity.

The learnings from these circles are that, varying very little by culture, women gather many wounds due to patriarchal neoliberal forces that come to them / us through parents, mothers, siblings, school, partners, doctors, etc., and leave traces in the body, mind, heart, and soul. We were able to recognize these wounds collectively starting from the first sessions on Gender (what is feminine and masculine and how we "learned" it), to the session on the sexualization of the body where we do a writing exercise (writing 3 different memories on our breasts) and watch a documentary on the topic, in our topics on menstruation, childbirth, and on motherhood as well.

The results of negative experiences are alienation from the body, alienation from the womb (which connects us to our foremothers and is a place for creativity, productivity, and joy and not a place of pain), mother-wounds, anger, grief, disappointment, and at times loss of own direction. On the topic of childbirth, after reading on the history of the medicalization of childbirth and watching the documentary "Born in the U.S.A." (Jarmel & Schneider, 2000) on hospital, birthing center and home births, we share on our experiences of childbirth and our responses to the readings and the documentary. Before that session, I ask the participants (if possible) to ask their mothers their own birthing story as well. During our circle, I read on childbirth in ancient cultures where childbirth includes more gentle, humane rituals and care where the women are treated with dignity and support, and the newborns (the new members of the community) are welcomed in joyful, honoring ways, in soft light and celebration. As we found in our research, of all the experiences shared on childbirth by women, very few are happy examples: most women (and their mothers) gave birth in either traumatic experiences or without consciousness or presence. I am always surprised by how women, the beings who can give birth (a miraculous sacred power), are treated with so little respect and care, during pregnancy and childbirth, and how society welcomes a new member in most cases with a traumatic experience rather than in a careful and joyful way.

Bringing It All Together, Closing the Circle with Future Visions: What Are Our Deepest Desires? What Can a Better Reproductive Care, Holistic Health and Healing Spaces Look Like?

If I may now try to integrate the academic and activist wisdom with the wisdom of Women's Circles, I can conclude that first there are multiple layers that have intersecting influences on women's sexuality and reproductive lives. As we saw from the research I shared here, state policies, neoliberal policies, neoconservativism, medicine and the level of medicalization, capitalist and neoliberal medicine, and reproductive technologies all impact women's sexual and reproductive lives and rights, and so far in quite a negative way. For women to feel fully empowered in their sexual and reproductive lives and services, and to be able to practice their human rights and flourish, all socioeconomic layers (state policies, economic policies, medical education and practice, and technological practices) need to be transformed to work in harmony.

At the moment, with all the age-long oppression of women, which has been mainly imposed through controlling women's sexuality and reproduction, my research, activism, and women's circles experience show that, due to these oppressive patriarchal measures that have intensified via neoliberal and neoconservative waves, for now, the women's deepest desires in terms of reproductive care center around safety (physical and emotional), dignity, and being able to practice their basic rights of privacy, freedom from violence, informed and non-judgmental, non-directive care. As in Maslow's stages of needs, first safety and basic human dignity need to be re-established for women, who then could be able to feel in control and flourish in their sexual and reproductive lives.

The experience of women who received care from Feminist Centers and of women in the women's circles give us how space for this flourishing can be. Women who have experienced care from the alternative, feminist centers and women who have come to my women's circles have recognized and cherish the qualities of a space that is not patriarchal and non-medical. These qualities of a non-medical, homey environment, a safe space, being treated with dignity, and in the case of women's circles, having a space to be able to freely explore one's femininity through movement, sharing, writing, meditation, may define important dimensions of a new reproductive care model for women. Hinted at also in Feminist Health Centers and experienced in women's circles, health and healing (be it reproductive or larger) needs to be holistic, addressing women as a whole person (not only in reproductive realm, not only through our wombs and reproductive systems but as a whole), and connecting body and mind, conscious and subconscious, where sexuality and reproduction (and reproductive life events or issues of dis-ease) are taken not as isolated issues but evaluated through the general mental, psychological, physical condition of the women. In this way, space can be created for women to heal through re-integrating, becoming whole again.

As a way of ending (which is hopefully a beginning of re-envisioning women's reproductive care in creative ways), I invite us to imagine a center where women can receive all reproductive care in one place, be it gynecological care/exams, contraception, abortion, and childbirth. I take to heart the Women's Health Movement's initial critique of mainstream, allopathic medicine, which is based on pathology (treating symptoms and disease). Only quite recently, in many countries, the more ancient medicine (i.e., Traditional Chinese Medicine) started to be incorporated into or taken alongside Western medicine in treatments. The Women's Health Movement advocates argued that because the Western medicine is based on pathology, and based on a patriarchal (and capitalist) system, women receiving care can only take the position of the patient (and doctors and nurses' knowledge are considered more important than women's own wisdom of their bodies). The advocates mentioned that this was not a proper model for reproductive care since experiencing menarche, menopause, birth control, abortion, or childbirth are normal life events (and not medical events to be medicalized and treated with unnecessary interventions), thus women are not sick but need care and support, with the appropriate use of medical and technological aid as needed. In the documentary I have used in teaching in academia and in women's circles, called Born in the U.S.A, on childbirth experience in the U.S.A, a midwife states that they are trained with the assumption that birth is a normal life event that many women, over ages, have accomplished with proper help and support, usually from other women, and that she treats the women as a whole and provides medical and hospital care when necessary. In contrast, the ob/gyn in the same movie, stated that they are trained as physicians and surgeons who are trained to focus on risk, on what could go wrong in pregnancy and birth, and to intervene (with technology) to "fix" it.

So, let us imagine places and spaces where women, from early ages, can learn about their sexuality and reproduction, from mothers, wise elderly women, teachers and health providers, and centers that utilize women's wisdom from perhaps holistic approaches that are making a come-back now, such as phytotherapy, movement (e.g., yoga and qigong), meditation, and through sharing of information on menses, contraceptive methods, abortion and childbirth in a non-medical way, where all services are given at the same center. I hope we can continue this imagination together.

References

Alkan, H., Dayi, A., Topçu, S., & Yarar, B. (2021). *The Politics of the female body in contemporary Turkey: Reproduction, maternity, sexuality.* Bloomsbury Publishing. https://www.bloomsbury.com/uk/the-politics-of-the-female-body-in-contemporary-turkey-9780755617401/

Casper, M. J. (1998). *The making of the unborn patient: A social anatomy of fetal surgery.* New Brunswick: Rutgers University Press.

Dayi, A. (2009). From power to safety and respect: The changing meaning of empowerment in women's reproductive health care in the US. *Fe Dergi, 1*(2), 53-70.

Dayi, A. (2011). Feminist centers negotiating medical authority in the 21st Century: Implications for feminist care and the US Women's Health Movement. In J.J. Kronenfeld (Ed.), *Access to care and factors that impact access, patients as partners in care and changing roles of health providers* (Vol. 29, pp. 197-228). Emerald Group Publishing Limited.

Dayi, A. (2019). Neoliberal health restructuring, neoconservatism and the limits of law: erosion of reproductive rights in Turkey. *Health and Human Rights, 21*(2), 57.

Dayi, A., & Karakaya, E. (2018). Transforming the gendered regime through reproductive politics: Neoliberal health restructuring, the debt economy and reproductive rights in Turkey. *Les Cahiers du CEDREF. Centre d'ensengnement, d'études et de Recherché pour les Études Féministes*, (22), 158-192. https://journals.openedition.org/cedref/1150.

Dayi, A., & Karakaya, E. (2021). Neoliberal health restructuring, rising conservatism and reproductive rights in Turkey: Continuities and changes in rights violations. In H. Alkan, A. Dayi, S.Topçu & B. Yarar (Eds.), *The politics of the female body in contemporary Turkey: Reproduction, maternity, sexuality* (pp. 17-42). Bloomsbury Publishing.

Duden, B. (1999). The fetus on the "farther shore": Toward a history of the unborn. In L.M. Morgan & M. W. Michaels (Eds.), *Fetal subjects, feminist positions* (pp. 13-25). Philadelphia: University of Pennsylvania Press.

Jarmel, M. & Schneider, K. (Directors) (2000). *Born in the U.S.A.* [Film]. Patchwork Films. IMDb. https://www.imdb.com/title/tt3670708/

Kapsalis, T. (2002). Mastering the female pelvis: Race and the tools of reproduction. In K. Wallace-Sanders (Ed.) *Skin deep, spirit strong: The black female body in American culture* (pp. 263-300). University of Michigan Press.

Leavitt, J. W. (1994). "Alone among strangers": The transition from home to hospital in American childbirth history. *International Journal of Childbirth Education, 9*(3), 5-7.

Leavitt, J. W. (2016). *Brought to bed: Childbearing in America, 1750-1950.* Oxford University Press.

Morgen, S. (2002). *Into our own hands: The women's health movement in the United States, 1969-1990.* New Brunswick: Rutgers University Press.

Roberts, D. E. (1998). *Killing the black body: Race, reproduction, and the meaning of liberty.* New York: Vintage Books.

Zimmerman, M. K., & Hill, S. A. (2000). Reforming gendered health care: an assessment of change. *International Journal of Health Services, 30*(4), 771-795.

Solidarity on a Thorny Road: Becoming a Feminist Psychologist in Turkey

Ayçe Feride Yılmaz

Yildiz Technical University, Istanbul, Turkey

Motivated by and aligned with the objectives of the Women's Liberation Movement for societal justice and transformation, feminist psychology has been extensively consolidated and formalized in North America and Western Europe. Throughout this process, it has provided thorough critiques on various aspects of mainstream psychological knowledge and practice (Marecek, 1995). Feminist psychologists have advocated for the shared responsibility of academic psychology in perpetuating the subordination of women by identifying and confronting the androcentric biases present in its subjects, research methodologies, and methods (Maccoby & Jacklin, 1974). Efforts have been made in the clinical field to challenge patriarchal cultural beliefs present in traditional psychoanalysis and to address the tendency of the clinical and psychiatric community to pathologize distress related to gender roles, oppressive sociopolitical structures, and patriarchal violence through diagnostic criteria and medical approaches (Ussher, 2019).

Furthermore, commencing in the 1970s, psychoanalytic feminism criticized classical psychoanalysis' psychosexual development model for its universalist, ahistorical, biologistic, and phallocentric tendencies. Psychoanalytic feminism encompasses a wide range of scholarship that aims to explore the constraints, deadlocks, and prospects within classical psychoanalysis (Benjamin, 1998; Irigaray, 1974/1985; Kamber, 2016; Kristeva, 1987; Mitchell, 1974). Utilizing primarily Freud's notion of the unconscious, its objective has been to revamp psychoanalytic theory by applying an emancipatory and empowering feminist perspective partially paving the way for the development of relational models of psychoanalysis (Eichenbaum & Obach, 2003). Relatedly, feminist psychoanalysis interrogates how feminist principles can inform clinical practice attending to the psychic effects of living under patriarchy (Baraitser, 2019).

Concomitantly, feminist therapy arising from feminist activism integrated political and private levels of analysis (Brown, 2018). Feminist therapists have challenged the use of classical psychoanalytic theory in reinforcing gendered norms that relegate women to domestic roles by pathologizing their desire for public engagement as neurotic, and by glorifying heterosexuality and motherhood as signs of maturity (Chesler, 2018; Friedan, 1963; Marecek & Hare-Mustin, 1991). Feminist therapy has developed a substantial body of theories, models, and various perspectives, and has become increasingly formalized through academic institutions, conferences, and publications (Brown, 2018; Evans et al., 2011). Furthermore, feminist therapists and activists have advocated for a critical examination of trauma theory, suggesting that the prevalence of physical and sexual violence in women's lives has been insufficiently acknowledged. They have argued that this issue should be viewed as a larger societal problem resulting from the cultural normalization of male dominance and social control. In the same way, feminist psychologists and therapists recognized further manifestations of gender-related trauma and devised corresponding interventions (Brown, 2017, 2018; Herman, 2015).

Given these extensive and versatile accomplishments spanning many decades in the West, little is known about the influence of feminist critical approaches in non-Western contexts. One such context is Turkey, where feminist clinical psychology is minimally represented yet holds significant importance within a deeply entrenched patriarchal cultural environment. Consequently, this study utilizes interviews conducted with four clinical practitioners who have openly identified themselves as feminist psychologists. These professionals maintain private practices and also work or volunteer at the Purple Roof (Mor Çatı) Women's Shelter Foundation in Istanbul, which is recognized as one of Turkey's pioneering and leading feminist organizations committed to advancing feminist politics and solidarity in opposition to gender-based violence. This study investigates how clinicians established their professional identities in alignment with feminist values and activism, as well as how they critically analyze their mainstream trainings.

The Feminist Movement and the Current Gender Politics in Turkey

Although women's civil and political rights were acknowledged by the Republic of Turkey in 1934, the country has not successfully eradicated entrenched cultural and social barriers that impede women's full participation in society, with the exception of a select few elite women (Çakır, 1994). Traditional gender norms, family relations, social segregation, and the policing of female sexuality remained prevalent, perpetuating women's subordination in both public and private spheres. Thus, although significantly moderated by regional and class differences, Turkish culture has overall preserved a collectivistic tone with close kinship and family ties based on patriarchal and authoritarian patterns that equate family honor with the control of women's sexuality and restrict their full public participation (Sunar & Fisek, 2005). A variety of forms of violence against women, including honor killings, underage forced marriages, and domestic violence, are prevalent within this constellation and are often perceived as culturally acceptable (Bora & Üstün, 2005). In cases of femicides, the extreme form and tool of hegemonic masculinity, "protecting honor", women's desire for divorce, their resistance to violence, pursuit of legal action, and questioning of masculinity and authority are among the supposed reasons for the killings (Afşar, 2016).

In an environment of suspended democratic rights and silenced political opposition, Turkey's second-wave feminism taking a more critical stance towards the state emerged in the aftermath of the 1980 military coup. These pioneering figures were mostly secular and educated women who had confronted sexism in their previous leftist political affiliations. Alternatively leaning towards socialist, radical, or liberal feminist positions, these groups launched the first public campaigns, marches, and protests to eliminate gender-based discrimination and violence. This included the petition drive in 1986 for the implementation of the United Nations Convention for the Elimination of All Forms of Discrimination Against Women (CEDAW), the first mass feminist demonstration in 1987 joined by 3000 women against domestic violence (sparked by a judge's refusal to grant a divorce based on a proverb legitimizing violence), and the Purple Needle Campaign in 1989, which comprised a series of protests, conferences, and parliamentary lobbying against sexual harassment (Arat, 2008; Diner & Tokaş, 2010). For the first time, uncovering and bringing to light these veiled and taboo violations in the public eye, these collective actions destabilized deep-rooted cultural and political assumptions, reducing domestic violence to a normalized private issue that is deemed irrelevant to social and political intervention, or in more modernist discourses, to an anomaly of some disturbed men or a social problem to be eliminated through progressive modernization (Boratav, 2011).

The third wave of feminism in the 1990s incorporated Kurdish and Islamist feminists, highlighting the differences and diversity of concerns amidst cleavages, as well as the need to explore potential alliances. The increasingly politicized Kurdish women's movement, pressing for a confrontation with nationalist ideology, also took on the task of illuminating and alleviating the harm inflicted on Kurdish women by the Kurdish-Turkish conflict. Ka-Mer, a prominent NGO founded during this period in the East and South East regions, additionally set forth to combat culturally sanctioned domestic violence and honor killings. The eve of this era was also marked by the establishment of several other prominent feminist NGOs, most notably the Purple Roof Women's Shelter Foundation highlighted in this article (Boratav, 2011).

Drawing on the concessional climate of the Europeanization process, the feminist movement played a critical role in influencing the state to enact the Domestic Violence Act in 1998 and make amendments to the Civil and Penal

Codes in 2001. These amendments removed articles that designated men as heads of households and conditioned women's work permission on their approval, while introducing key articles to increase punishments for gender-based violence, sexual harassment, sex crimes, and marital rape (Arat, 2023).

The enactment of such legislative measures attests to the increasingly consolidated status of the feminist movement. However, the implementation of laws on gender-based violence and constitutional indemnities has remained perpetually inadequate and inert, crystallizing the male-dominated state apparatus' sanctioning of traditional gender roles and socio-cultural norms (Yalcinoz-Ucan, 2022). Exceeding the enduring stance of inertia, the current government's gender politics - described as neo-patrimonial or neoliberal-patriarchal governance - alarmingly signal a reversal of gains against gender-based violence. The most dramatic example of this conjuncture was Turkey's arbitrary withdrawal from the Council of Europe's Istanbul Convention on Preventing and Combating Violence against Women and Domestic Violence in 2021, which triggered similar debates concerning the abolishment of national law 6284 on Protection of Family and Prevention of Violence against Women. Even before the withdrawal, there was a lack of will to properly administer the convention's requirements, as evidenced by the limited number of shelters primarily located in urban areas and the failure of police and local law enforcement mechanisms to follow legal steps in cases of domestic violence (Ekal, 2017; Kara et al. 2014; Toktas & Diner, 2015). This configuration results in the proliferation of domestic violence, afflicting 39% of women nationwide, and the rise of femicides that had befallen 2,641 women between 2016 and 2023 (We Will Stop Femicides Platform, n.d.). Coupled with critical factors such as lack of income and housing, these systemic barriers are significantly implicated in women's entrapment in violent marriages and relationships, leading to their reluctance to disclose violence and seek formal support (Akadli-Ergocmen et al., 2013; Alan et al., 2016).

Thus, relying on the socio-political and cultural realm in Turkey, patriarchal ideology continues to prevail, resulting in male abuse and violence against women being seen as a private and culturally acceptable matter. Additionally, while ostensibly condemning violence against women as a violation of human rights in line with the UN declarations, the government structurally and socio-culturally perpetuates a conservative climate by promoting religious education, pro-familial policies, and social policy transformations that shift state responsibilities to women's caregiving roles (Çağatay, 2019).

As one of the precursors and strongholds of feminist mobilization for combating male violence using feminist principles and methods, the Purple Roof Women's Shelter Foundation, founded in 1990, continues to stand out as a fundamental agent of feminist politics in the face of this deteriorating landscape. The Purple Roof has been providing vital protection and shelter services, guided by feminist principles, through volunteer-led social work, legal assistance, and psychological support for women and children. The organization extends its reach through its solidarity center (Arat, 1994; Bora & Günal, 2002). In terms of its broader agenda of feminist politics, the Purple Roof engages in campaigns and collaborations with national and international women's organizations. It also organizes workshops and fosters partnerships with bar associations, municipalities, NGOs, universities, and other women's organizations to convey awareness-raising information and share experiences derived from feminist solidarity work. Furthermore, in addition to monitoring the implementation of national and international legislations, conventions, and by-laws aimed at combatting violence against women and promoting gender equality, policymakers are presented with proposals for meaningful policy changes.

All operations in the foundation are carried out through non-hierarchical, egalitarian, and collective efforts, reflected in the rotation of authorizations and responsibilities, simultaneously with discussion-based decision-making. Having a diverse network of volunteers from various professions and sectors allows for access to any practical or material needs. The Purple Roof also supports social responsibility initiatives of multiple corporations (Yılmaz, 2020).

In addition to several workshops, group and social work on gender inequality, forms of patriarchal violence, and behaviors, individual psychological support extended to women and their children for a period of six months to one year is one of the major components of integrative solidarity. The ongoing efforts of psychologists associated with feminist psychological perspectives are notable, especially when considering the scarcity of resources in contrast to the predominant market-driven institutionalization of psychology and psychoanalysis discussed below.

The Lack of Critical and Feminist Influences on Psychology and Psychoanalysis in Turkey

The development and growth of modern psychology took place in the late Ottoman Empire and the young Turkish Republic between 1915 and 1945 under strong German influence (Acar & Şah, 1990). As part of changing political alliances starting in the 1950s, the US positivist mainstream psychology and the cognitive-behaviorist school of thought have replaced the early European influence and have been primarily followed to this day in Turkish academia and professional training. Over the last few decades, psychology has attracted immense popularity, with many undergraduate and graduate programs opening at private universities (Aslıtürk & Batur, 2014; Sümer, 2016). Pursuing graduate-level psychology education to become a clinical practitioner is the primary motive for much of this growing interest, although the number of graduate-level programs is still insufficient to meet this demand.

In order to survive the competitive circumstances in the market, many candidates consider clinical and other applied areas of mainstream psychology as offering lucrative financial prospects. Moreover, they participate in multiple certificate programs offered by profit-oriented private universities or professional associations in addition to their formal education. This landscape is the socio-economic outcome of the neoliberal restructuring and privatization process of the economy ongoing since the 1980s, which has co-opted the education system (Kayaoğlu & Batur, 2013). These developments result in the prioritization of profit over quality of care and the perpetuation of the lack of attention to critical and feminist perspectives.

Psychiatrists still play a key role in the mental health system as sole authorities for prescribing medication. Nevertheless, rising pop psychology trends disseminated through TV programs, self-help books, and print media have generated significant interest and demand for privatized psychological services. These services are primarily accessible to urban middle or upper classes, unlike the lower segments who are unable to access such well-known and desired services while navigating structural financial fragility (Kayaoğlu & Batur, 2013; Sümer, 2016).

However, beginning in the 2000s, these significant changes have also given rise to a cohort of politically engaged and critically minded psychologists who are increasingly voicing social critiques against conventional mainstream psychology, associated academic institutions, professional organizations, and privately operated mental health services. These circles with leftist leanings incrementally expanded their endeavors, ultimately leading to the foundation of the Psychologists for Social Solidarity Association (TODAP)(Kayaoğlu & Batur, 2013). Incorporating a feminist-oriented Women's Unit, TODAP is one of the few institutions where critical psychological knowledge, including feminist psychology, is circulated. Therefore, the participants of this study are also commonly affiliated with it.

In the clinical sphere, a few psychiatrists and psychologists, as vanguard figures of the second and third-wave women's movement, initiated criticism of androcentric clinical approaches. They also introduced international feminist insights relevant to gender-based violence, sexual abuse, and incest, and played major roles in establishing and consolidating the Purple Roof (Güneri, 1996; Yüksel, 1995). They were joined by other pioneering therapist activists and therapist academics who contributed to the understanding and questioning of gender-based violence and forms of abuse in socio-cultural terms (Fişek,1990; İlkkaracan & İlkkaracan, 1998). Influenced or trained by these few vanguard figures, and/or affiliated with the TODAP, Purple Roof, and other feminist organizations, a minor group of feminist psychologists from younger generations accordingly endorse and implement feminist therapeutic perspectives.

Parallel to mainstream psychology education and training, a similar apolitical and acultural orthodoxy prevails concerning psychoanalysis and psychoanalytical training in Turkey. Psychoanalysis has emerged belatedly and is in an inadequately developed state in comparison to Western contexts. Islam and segregated gender relations in society, which contradict psychoanalysis' conventional associations with sexuality, atheism, and unconscious determinism, along with a lack of complete transition to Western autonomous selfhood and nationhood tied to top-down and non-linear modernization and secularization, seem to play a part in this hindered encounter (Gülerce, 2008).

Nevertheless, based on economic and social globalization fostering the expansion of Western liberal values, including Western autonomous selfhood, in the 1990s, interest in psychoanalysis started to intensify and was sought after by affluent urban social segments (Gülerce, 2008). Both parts of the International Psychoanalytical Association - the Istanbul Psychoanalytical Association, founded in 2001, and Psike Istanbul (Association for the Training, Research, and Development of Psychoanalysis), established in 2003 - are two major institutions that offer official analysis, training, and supervision for candidate analysts according to mainstream international standards. The Istanbul Child and Adolescent Psychoanalytic Psychotherapy Association, established in 2006, offers training based on the European Federation of Psychoanalytic Psychotherapy.

Materials and Method

Study objectives

This investigation reports on a qualitative study conducted with four Turkish women who identify as feminist psychologists and are currently working or volunteering at the Purple Roof Women's Shelter Foundation. The study questions being tackled are: I) "How did participants consolidate their professional identities in relation to their feminist values and activism?" II) "How did they come to problematize their mainstream educations and clinical trainings, or expand on them?" The research questions are designed to explore how participants interpret, view, and undergo the process of becoming feminist psychologists. The premise is that, as important actors promoting feminist psychology in Turkey, their stories may illuminate major fault-lines of decontextualized and apolitical mainstream approaches and highlight the vitality of underrepresented feminist-oriented clinical work to adequately respond to socio-cultural and political patriarchy.

Participants and Recruitment Process

The sampling criteria for this study required participants to have an open feminist psychologist identity and to work or volunteer at the Purple Roof. This ensures they possess extensive knowledge and experience in practicing therapy with feminist principles and are involved in feminist politics. I knew three of the participants from having met them as colleagues primarily at TODAP events over the years. One participant, whom I had not known before, was approached through the mediation of another participant. The participation of all attendees in this study was confirmed by the Purple Roof's collective body, which is composed of 20 women responsible for executing all matters of the foundation through egalitarian discussion and consensus-based decision-making.

All participants are female and reside in Istanbul. Their ages range from 35 to 45. All of them have a BA in Psychology and are in private practice. Participant 1 holds an MA in Trauma Studies and another MA in Women's Studies. Participant 2 has a master's degree in Trauma and Disaster Studies, while Participant 3 has a master's degree in Psychology. Participant 4 is continuing her master's degree in clinical psychology.

At the Purple Roof, Participants 1 and 4 work with adult women, while Participants 2 and 3 work with children and adolescents. Participant 3 also works online for a symbolic fee at a feminist NGO in the eastern part of Turkey, where patriarchy is deeply rooted and strong.

Participant 1 describes her clinical work as feminist psychotherapy, primarily utilizing trauma-informed and (supportive) psychodynamic frameworks. She participates in psycho-dynamically oriented supervision with a professional who aligns with feminist ideology and engages in feminist therapy for personal growth. Participant 2 characterizes her work as aligned with psychoanalytical and psychodynamic principles within the context of feminist psychology. She has been engaging in self-analysis, receiving guidance from psychoanalyst supervisors, and attending seminars at accredited institutes. Participant 3 describes her work as psychoanalytically oriented therapy that incorporates feminist principles and receives psychoanalytic supervision. Participant 4 describes herself as a feminist psychotherapist with a psychoanalytic orientation. She has been actively participating in psychoanalytic and psychodynamic seminars, as well as informal trainings, while also undergoing self-analysis and receiving supervision from an analyst. Following their collaboration at the Purple Roof, she continues to work with some of her clients for only symbolic fees. Participants 2, 3, and 4 are not yet analysts and describe their work as psychoanalytically oriented.

Interview Procedures

Participants were provided with an explanation of the study objectives, and their informed consent for participation and recording was obtained in written format through email correspondence. All of them indicated they viewed their participation as a contribution to feminist research, solidarity, and dissemination of feminist ideals. Notarized documents, including my commitment to erase the recordings, were promised to be delivered to them. They were informed that their names would not appear in the manuscript unless they accepted the co-authorship offered to them, which they declined. This study assumes a feminist methodology, explicitly putting forth the researcher's values of collaboration and participatory process, in terms of opening the researcher's interpretations and data to participant modification and removal (Beckman, 2014). Therefore, in line with feminist principles, they were informed that they would be able to review the final version of this study and make any necessary revisions or additions to both the information provided and interpretations. This procedure was subsequently carried out.

Interviews lasting between 50 and 90 minutes were conducted via Zoom. The first question in the interviews was, "Can you tell me the story of your journey to becoming a feminist psychologist?" This allowed participants to share their narrations in a non-intrusive manner. For ethical reasons, participants were informed that they could start their story with the life phase of their choice and provide personal details as they saw fit. They were told they can share anything that made them the feminist psychologists that they are today. After participants completed their narration, they were asked additional, more direct questions to clarify ambiguities or extract more detail related to the themes they brought up. The interviews were conducted in Turkish and translated by the author into English. Participants agreed to the accuracy of the translations.

Data Analysis

As a descriptive and interpretive endeavor, this study does not aim to produce objective and generalizable findings. Instead, utilizing Interpretative Phenomenological Analysis (IPA), it focuses on how participants make sense of their life experiences, generating themes that are linked to the researchers' interpretations (Pietkiewicz & Smith, 2014). Although, the IPA approach gives an active interpretative role to the researcher, in line with IPA studies that incorporate feminist approaches (Cohen et al, 2022), I prioritize participants' interpretations to align with feminist principles of voice-giving. It is presumed that, in addition to their personal histories, participants' narratives would also reveal the socio-cultural and political-structural dynamics of Turkey. This would highlight the factual importance and utility of feminist clinical work in empowering recipients.

In IPA, small and homogeneous samples are favored for detailed examination, aligning with the sample size of this study. Each interview transcription was carefully reviewed and analyzed multiple times. At the outset, handwritten exploratory notes were recorded to document all descriptions, ideas, comments, key words, and questions alongside the text segments. The preliminary notes facilitated a thoughtful examination of the data, enabling my discernment to accurately capture the perspectives and experiences of each participant. The preliminary notes served as the basis for developing emergent themes, which are interpretive summaries for distinct parts of the text and indicate a higher-level conceptual framework. In order to identify the relationships among emergent themes, they were categorized into clusters that comprised the overarching personal themes at a higher level of conceptualization. This procedure was conducted for every participant. In IPA, cross-case analysis is typically presented as a means of demonstrating similarities and differences among participants. However, in order to convey the unique richness of each life story, this study opted to present individual case analyses.

Reflexivity

As a feminist social psychologist and a woman who has experienced gender-based violence, I view this research as part of the solidarity within the feminist movement in Turkey. It allows me to give a voice to activist psychologists' subjectivities, highlighting their meanings and efforts, which form the basis of my overarching methodological framework. I acknowledge that my political, cultural, and experiential beliefs and values influence my perspective on this research from a feminist standpoint.

During the research process, I employed memo-writing to facilitate my analytical and emotional processing of the interview experiences and materials alongside my potential influence on the research process. In these memos, I often reflected on my own history in terms of similarities and differences in personal and professional life experiences, as well as the accompanying emotions. I also scrutinized my ethical positionality by gathering life stories involving sensitive material to understand how I was influencing my participants and what I could do to make the process more ethical. For example, although there was no major power imbalance or detached objectivism, as is often seen in positivistic research, I found that listening to material that resonated with my personal and professional experiences was challenging. I experienced the implicit difficulty of maintaining a relatively detached researcher and listener role. This led me to a feminist strategy of mutuality and power reduction. That is, I sometimes engaged in complementary dialogue and, at other times, in self-disclosure.

Results

The results section follows a participant-by-participant analysis of the research questions: I) "How did feminist psychologists consolidate their professional identities in relation to feminist values and activism?" II) "How did they problematize their mainstream educations and/or expand upon them?"

Participant 1: Propelled by Activism and the Field: Gropingly but Persistently Searching for Feminist Psychology

Participant 1's life narrative is marked by a pursuit of a feminist psychologist identity on a dim path. That is, it is a story of constant and progressive pursuits amidst the discontents stemming from the incompatibility of her feminist beliefs with her conventional education and training.

Dissatisfactions and Alerting Flares while Becoming a Feminist

Participant 1 reflects on her mainstream psychology education, recognizing its limitations in retrospect. Looking from a distance, she realizes much more clearly the unsatisfactory quality of it and how she was merely alerted to some alternative insights she had always been looking for but could never pinpoint, by two courses on cultural psychology and social responsibility.

> "I said, -Wait a minute, there is something else here-. I slimly began to see that there is a counterpart to something I always lacked but could never name. Some connection between gender and mental health."

Another major alerting sign for Participant 1 was her haphazard encounter with the concept of womb envy in a conventional psychology book that challenges the male-centered theories and models of mainstream psychology to which she had been exposed.

> "Encountering Horney's concept of womb envy by happenstance in a conventional personality psychology book was very surprising to me. I remember feeling such a thrill and being so enchanted by it. Because I have always felt a significant, unnamed discomfort with phallocentric theories."

The opportunities presented by these encounters appear to intersect with and give depth to her negative experiences as a young woman in her family, along with her early efforts in exploring feminist mobilizations.

> "During the same years, I began to identify myself as a feminist. Outside of school, I began attending meetings of feminist organizations and Purple Roof. I was questioning gender roles because of the experiences I had at home. But I still did not know anything about feminist psychology or therapy."

Fostered by her feminist activism, Participant 1 starts working at a municipal shelter for women exposed to violence after graduation. Once again, due to the intertwining of these two enlightening experiences, she increasingly appreciates how her apolitical and decontextualized psychology education largely failed to acknowledge the realities in the field, leading to her frustrations becoming more pronounced.

> "I saw there how the mainstream formation was not working and what it left out. I felt a deep sense of restriction and congestion, especially considering that I am a feminist. I did not go into the field with the ambition of becoming a feminist psychologist, but I discovered its vitality there."

During this period, Participant 1 appears to clearly identify the problematic aspects and areas mainstream approaches overlook, recognizing how, as authoritative knowledge forms, they contribute to the social construction and reiteration of misogyny.

> "I saw that clinical work without a feminist method may serve to reproduce social myths. For example, explaining a woman's self-blame after being exposed to sexual violence as a result of internal conflicts or object relations, while omitting the immense social baggage... Disregarding the fact that the misogynistic victim-blaming socio-cultural configuration leads women to take this blame upon themselves in the first place and dismissing the social counterpart of this emotion..."

This suggests that Participant 1 comes to view mainstream interpretations and interventions as stubbornly turning a blind eye to the patriarchal violence that induces psychological distress and thinks through their individual-level theories and models, they become complicit in essentializing and implicitly pathologizing the patriarchal harm inflicted on victims. It is also noteworthy that Participant 1 shifts to the plural pronoun form, indicating that she understands the shortcomings of mainstream approaches not solely factually, or does not employ the stance of a distanced clinician, but identifies with women and stands against the pathologization of the perpetrators.

> "Overlooking that, we, women experience and learn to self-blame throughout our lives on many fronts, constantly bombarded with victim-blaming accusations... Explaining perpetrators' acts of violence against us based on their personal traumas or pathologies... Mainstream approaches were fraught with such blind spots and pitfalls."

Participant 1 enrolls in a clinically oriented mainstream master's program in trauma studies, taught mainly by psychiatrists, feeling obligated to obtain a degree in order to become a practicing professional. Although disappointed, Participant 1 notes that she can still be considered lucky since she had already entered the field and started volunteering as a feminist.

> "In fact, looking back, I think conducting trauma studies without politicizing trauma requires great effort. But then, I had the chance to somewhat alleviate this scarcity since I was actively involved on the ground as a feminist and volunteering."

This delineates the extent of the disconnect she sees between the effects of patriarchal realities on psychological well-being, which she witnesses on the ground, and conventional academic knowledge and clinical practice. Additionally, this quote signals that she considers the knowledge coming from the field that she integrates into a feminist framework to be more guiding and nurturing.

Searching Persistently for Feminist Scholarship

Intent on discovering the scholarship she had only sporadically been able to contact, Participant 1 decides to pursue another master's degree in women's studies. Here she taps into the field of feminist psychology with a sense of fulfillment.

> "I did not even know how to find the feminist psychological compendia I was yearning for. So, for the first time, I felt an amazing sense of satisfaction, happiness, and belonging. Reading the works of contemporary feminist psychologists on violence and the critiques of psychoanalysis..."

The following quote further emphasizes a concomitant melancholy that accompanies her enthusiasm, as she comes to the realization that her self-doubts were not only baseless but truly valid, backed up by decades of scholarship and activism that are overlooked in mainstream trainings. This demonstrates that formal psychology education programs can create barriers of uncertainty for inquisitive and analytical minds. This experience seems to integrate the theoretical gaps in her mind by strongly connecting the knowledge from her field experiences, feminist activism, and feminist psychological scholarship, while also specifying the structural nature of gender-based violence.

> "I also felt a bit sad, as during my isolated questioning, I had felt marginalized, without a counterpart, and even absurd. On the contrary, I saw that there is a comprehensive collection spanning many decades, featuring women's inquiries. The limited connections in my mind started to come together, illuminating conclusively that violence is a patriarchal phenomenon, not an issue of anger management or pathology."

Pushing for Identity among Insecurities

After accessing the feminist psychological compendia following a long academic and activist journey, Participant 1 states that she has become increasingly convinced that feminist psychology and therapy align with her values and professional goals. Nevertheless, as she is positioned within an overwhelmingly mainstream professional milieu, this environment insidiously instils self-doubt in her.

> "I remember writing a piece for a journal criticizing orthodox psychoanalysis and arguing that the therapy room is a political space. But at the same time, I was feeling tremendously insecure and uneasy while seeking confirmation from colleagues. While pursuing feminist psychology, I went through many internal pains and struggles, questioning whether I was doing something wrong, whether my feminist and psychologist identities were incompatible, and whether my identity as a feminist psychologist would adversely affect my clients."

She tries to counteract these insecurities by conversing and affiliating with a few like-minded colleagues. Her comment below, on her friend's supervisor's contradictory remark, exemplifies how she eventually combines her feminist and psychologist identities to the point where they have become an integral part of her.

> "One time, while exchanging our questionings with a colleague, she mentioned that her supervisor had instructed her to decide between becoming an activist or a therapist. I was perplexed by the absurdity of this statement, as it seemed to me to be just as ridiculous as leaving one's arm behind the therapy room. Afterwards, I became quite convinced of my position, yet my need for confirmation nevertheless persisted."

This quote also implies that the hurdles she encounters in the mainstream community paradoxically both destabilize her confidence and provide a continuing ambition to pursue her position.

Identity Consolidation as an Activist and a Feminist Psychologist

Participant 1 ambitiously persists in overcoming and clarifying her confusions by consulting with a few pioneering feminist psychiatrists in Turkey, reading and attending Judit Herman's speeches, and reaching out to international feminist therapists. They tell her that, for a feminist psychologist, concealing her identity was pointless. Beginning employment at the Purple Roof serves as a definitive turning point that solidifies her position.

> "Step by step, especially after starting to work at the Purple Roof, I overcame my insecurity. Now, being able to openly say that I am a feminist therapist is a luxury to me, a point reached after enduring so much pain. The transformation brought to me by the Purple Roof is the ability to embrace my identity as a feminist psychologist and apply the principles of feminist therapy in my work."

Nevertheless, in addition to embracing her identity as a feminist psychologist, Purple Roof is closely linked to the larger agenda of engaging in feminist politics and activism in solidarity, which is also personally empowering for her.

> "But psychological support is just one component of our feminist solidarity. Feminism is also integrated into our entire body of work. I do not define my work as clinical, but as part of solidarity. Not only as a psychologist, but also as a feminist continuing to fight against the system in general, I find strength. Because otherwise, one truly feels stuck and helpless."

Overall, navigating the distressing ambiguity of tapping into feminist psychological knowledge within an ungerminated social and intellectual context leads Participant 1 to enhance her mainstream training through feminism in alternative academic settings. Coupled with her activism and field work, this participant becomes increasingly convinced that feminism infused into psychological work is vital and viable. However, she still navigates intense self-doubts amid the mainstream professional circles' entrenchment, resolving both internal and external roadblocks and tensions. In particular, starting work at the Purple Roof culminates in her conclusively claiming this identity intertwined with her feminist activism.

Participant 2: Rejecting the Mainstream and the Misogyny within Psychological Knowledge and Practice

Participant 2 currently works with children and adolescents at the Purple Roof. Although like Participant 1, her consolidation of her feminist identity and disillusionment with her mainstream psychology training went very parallel, she takes a more direct approach to rejecting mainstream ideas and challenging misogynistic views in psychological knowledge and practice.

Becoming a Feminist and Early Dissatisfactions

Participant 2 comes from a smaller town to Istanbul for her university education and soon embarks on a process of individuation, building an independent life. This enables her to look from a distance at her family dynamics, spotting and scrutinizing the inequalities more closely. Affiliating with like-minded feminists at her university, Participant 2 simultaneously struggles with her family in her hometown to assert her mobility and independence. These experiences, combined with her growing awareness of gender inequality, led her to identify as a feminist.

She soon starts to question what she can do both personally to cultivate her consciousness and contribute politically, seeking options for feminist mobilizations. This leads her to attend Purple Roof's general discussions, which resemble consciousness-raising groups. Particularly regarding male violence, these groups deepen her understanding of her own experiences by pointing out painful blind spots she was not able to discern in the past, and enhance her commitment to be part of the struggle against this violence.

> "Participating in these groups on various topics helped me discover myself and had a positive impact on me. Additionally, they helped me gain awareness of male violence, making me realize how uninformed I had been and how I had been exposed to it in my family and relationships."

Around this time, at the beginning of her undergraduate education in mainstream psychology, Participant 2, a new student exploring the discipline, does not fully embrace a critically oppositional perspective. However, she does have the chance to take a course from a feminist teacher in social psychology while also affiliating with TODAP. During her master's training in Trauma and Disaster Studies, she feels a growing dissatisfaction with mainstream psychology.

> "I felt the discomfort and congestion of mainstream approaches more clearly. There were teachers supporting and collaborating with the state's family centers to provide anger management services for violent men. I remember one teacher, who also happened to collaborate with these centers, proclaiming that the anger voiced by feminism was nonsensical and could not be related in any way to the therapy work."

These elements set the stage for her feminist outlook when entering the clinical field as a trainee and later as a practitioner.

Not Taking-in the Mainstream

During these years of her master training and early clinical practice, while attending seminars at psychoanalytic institutes and receiving supervision, comments by her teachers and supervisors regarding the incompatibility of her feminist and psychologist identities induce a short-lived reservation in Participant 2. She attributes this hesitancy to the perceived authority of mainstream psychology and psychoanalysis, rather than a change in her feminist beliefs. Yet, as Participant 2 delves more deeply into feminist psychological literature and witnesses stalemates that mainstream psychological knowledge cannot address, she increasingly becomes more forthright and stands up for her position as a feminist psychologist while affiliating with only a few colleagues.

> "As I gained experience and became more familiar with contemporary discussions in feminist psychology, encountering knots and seeing things that did not work with mainstream knowledge, my initial hesitancy did not last long. An opening emerged upon seeing feminist psychology's interpretations, which also granted me courage and strength. Through readings and conversations with a few other feminist colleagues, we explored how feminist psychology might be possible in practice..."

Participant 2's accounts exemplify the extent of misogynistic influence within the clinical establishment, particularly in regards to clinicians' tendency to blame mothers and women. From a certain point onwards, Participant 2 opposes and directly problematizes patriarchal versions of clinical knowledge and practice, especially within psychoanalytic and psychodynamic communities.

> "Classical psychoanalysis can interpret it like this, or a theoretical educator can argue that there must be clear gender roles, wherein the child receives both mother's care and father's authority. In cases of sexual violence against children, analytic professionals may raise direct arguments blaming the mother for not being able to adequately protect, take care of, or acknowledge the violation."

Participant 2 is able to aptly problematize mother-shaming or pathologizing tendencies in psychoanalytic communities by linking such misogynistic accusations to a decontextualized ignorance of the overwhelming violence against women.

> "In psychoanalytic and psychodynamic communities, it is common to make inferences about a certain phenomenon solely by blaming the mother. With minds directly wandering there, mother supposedly being borderline, bipolar or careless, responsible for insecure, avoidant attachment... Then again, why does the mother experience difficulties? Why does she attach to her child in an insecure way? What is she exposed to from the father? And what about the father's neglect of the child? The mother may be exposed to severe violence, even be on the verge of being killed, but she still must treat her child in a certain way and be omnipotent."

Participant 2's agency is also reflected in her opposition to and removal from misogynistic people and institutions, as well as her refusal to incorporate such teachings and views into her own practice.

> "I worked briefly with the child of a woman who was exposed to severe physical violence, almost to the point of murder. My supervisor made this comment: 'How did this woman let herself get beaten up. How couldn't she say no?' I could not go on very long with that person. From a certain point onward, I voiced my criticisms, oppositions, and disagreements in group settings. In my practice, I did not take those things in and, in the therapy room, these experiences caused me to increasingly side with mothers and women."

Participant 2's position is fully consolidated in the right environment, with her volunteering experience at the Purple Roof, as explained below.

Consolidating the Feminist Psychologist Identity through the Purple Roof

During this time, Participant 2 starts volunteering at the Purple Roof, which she describes as a turning point in her life and for her identity as a feminist psychologist. Having already clearly established her standing, Participant 2 seamlessly integrates her feminist, psychologist, and activist identities by performing her profession within a feminist political organization where she feels a sense of belonging. For Participant 2, feminist egalitarian solidarity against gender-based violence provides hope for change and transformation for all involved, including herself.

> "Building solidarity among women has resulted in numerous changes, both in the lives of volunteers and in the lives of the women and children with whom we stand in solidarity. An opening, a path, a door for change..."

She extends her hope for making a difference and her solidarity efforts, components of her feminist psychologist identity, to both her private practice and to her work in feminist politics at the Purple Roof.

> "This extends outside of my clinic when accepting clients from now on. Having this identity has led me to filter and critically analyze every narrative that is shared with me. Feminist knowledge consistently emerges in practice through listening to women's experiences, the violence and abuse children endure, and the inequalities perpetuated by the patriarchy. I am able to apply this knowledge to politics at the Purple Roof."

Participant 2's account underscores numerous misogynistic fault lines within mainstream educational and professional circles, as well as her opposition to and navigation of those issues. It also reveals how, amidst such unsuitable contexts and meagre resources, strong-minded pursuits can culminate in confi-

Becoming a Feminist Psychologist in Turkey 93

dently embracing and implementing a feminist psychological position. The hope and zeal in Participant 2's narration concerning making a change in terms of violence against women are exemplify the opportunities feminist psychology offers for challenging contexts like Turkey.

Participant 3: A Life Story Constituting a Stronghold for Feminism

Participant 3 first worked as a social worker and currently volunteers as a psychologist for children and adolescents at the Purple Roof. She recognizes that she values feminism as a responsibility to herself, her society, and her profession. She also holds a private practice and works at an NGO in a city in the eastern part of Turkey where patriarchy is deeply entrenched and strong.

Participant 3 comes from an Alevite family and community. Alevites are heterodox non-Sunni Islamic ethno-religious communities, estimated to make up between 10 and 15% of Turkey's total population. They uphold relatively gender-equitable ways of life, moral teachings, and ceremonies (Açikel & Ateş, 2011). Her childhood environment involved a quite liberal way of upbringing; nevertheless, it also signals poignant contradictions within the community as a context that is not free of patriarchy and gender-based violence.

A "Free Childhood" Infiltrated by Patriarchy

Growing up in an Alevite neighborhood in a small city, Participant 3 stresses that she did not feel women's oppression in her own nuclear family, as her mother was a dominant woman and her father was a soft-hearted man. Yet, she quickly adds that she had not been able to discern subtle details, such as her father coming home late while her mother could not, or that he was more in charge of monetary matters. Until adolescence, she could play freely late at night on the streets, while her Sunni friends could not and were instead forced to do house chores. Even in adolescence, when her whereabouts were occasionally questioned, it was enough for her to say she was bicycling.

Even in her relatively egalitarian family, remnants of intergenerational patriarchal thinking, as well as the stronger influence of patriarchy in previous generations of Alevite communities, were evident, as illustrated by the quote below about her family's and her mother's contradictions.

> "On one hand, they were supporting our freedom, but on the other hand, they were afraid that I could be harmed."

> "Although my mother was not able to show her love too much, she had taken an oath as she had been raised in a way that pressured her to stay indoors, do house-

work, and not go outside to play. She said, 'My children will not be interrupted while playing and can be outside as much as they want.' Yet now, she says to me that she regrets letting me be too free, as I became a feminist who goes around as an 'overly liberated woman,' which makes me laugh..."

Despite the community's egalitarian reputation, the contradictions afflicting her nuclear family also seem to arise from the societal patriarchy that permeates women's mindsets. She also identifies this configuration as a contributing factor to her wrong marriage, prompting her to engage in emotional reflection.

"My mother warned us against having boyfriends in our provincial city due to rumors we heard from the neighbor women about girls with boyfriends... That they were stained, bad, and unfit for marriage... Obviously, my mind received the message that one cannot experience sexuality before marriage. This was a factor for me in making a very poor decision to marry at a young age and have two children."

Although on the surface, her nuclear family arrangements may appear nonoppressive towards her, Participant 3 grows up listening to the traumatic experiences her grandmother endured since a very young age. This reveals how the patriarchy entrenched in previous generations gradually influenced her as a woman when she started discovering feminism.

"Looking back, I realized that listening to her traumatic stories since the age of 3 had left a lasting impact on my subconscious, burdening me emotionally. Consequently, she had a profound influence on my subconscious transformation into a feminist."

Participant 3's grandmother, having spent her younger years in a much more conservative social context, was forced to marry at a young age. She attempted to hang herself, but was prevented by her brothers, who harshly beat her. Participant 3 emphasizes the dramatic nature of this violence by noting that her grandmother used to show them her crushed skull. One of the most drastic stories centers on her grandmother getting her period at 9 and being violently beaten by her mother with firewood due to suspicion of rape. This results in Participant 3's fearful reaction to her own period, as evidenced by her screaming, staying in bed for several days, and walking as if crippled. She translates this story, decoding the ingrained patriarchal messages.

"I used to listen to these stories hundreds of times since the age of 3. My grandmother's telling of this story had a message that I believe was discouraging us from engaging in sexual activities, as it seemed to resonate with me by equating womanhood with bloodshed and horror."

Hearing about the murders of her neighbor and their tenant by their husbands were other influential events that enforced the stamp of patriarchy on her childhood. Of note, these landmark emotional events are preserved by the participant without an explicit connection to feminist (psychological) theories. However, once encountering this knowledge, they provide the affective fuel necessary for integration into intellectual feminist philosophies.

> "All of these experiences have made me a feminist with strong convictions... The tremendous oppression... Back then, these experiences did not make me a feminist, but when I encountered feminism, it strongly resonated with me because I had already witnessed women's oppression, the suppression of sexuality, and violence..."

As illustrated below, her marriage, as an embodied experience, seems to provide the cornerstone event and transformative life phase for embracing feminism and becoming a feminist psychologist.

A Patriarchal Marriage Culminating in Feminism

When she reaches that part of her story, she emotionally distances herself by saying it is a long story and can be skipped. Although she subsequently specifies details such as economic violence, control, imposition of household labor, and devaluation, the author has omitted these components, focusing primarily on the consolidation of her feminist awareness within her marriage.

> "Identifying the existence and prevalence of psychological violence even in the absence of physical violence... I noticed and fully realized women's oppression. That women are intentionally placed at a disadvantaged position by men, society, and the state, with men benefiting immensely from this..."

Her usage of the plural pronoun form and her reference to various patriarchal actors in the above quote further substantiate that she was already able to make feminist connections and analyses. After getting a divorce and quitting her job, she enters the feminist movement, starts working at the Purple Roof as a social worker, and engages with feminist psychology through TODAP. The fact that she went about so consciously and intently to take these steps indicates that she has already formulated a self-informed feminist mindset.

A Feminist in a Feminist Utopia in Solidarity

By joining the feminist movement and becoming affiliated with TODAP, Participant 3 has the opportunity to gain extensive knowledge about feminist psychology from colleagues. Soon after, she begins working at the Purple Roof, where her social work incorporates her psychological knowledge and resembles counselling. Above all, she comes to appreciate the integrative support that goes beyond psychology, involving essential practical and material needs.

> "There, I had the chance to go beyond psychology through a more holistic approach. We were able to assist a woman with her entire life, including helping her

find a job and a house, as well as providing all the necessary support for her children. Even while going to the bar and having fun, women were able to leave their children and reintegrate into social life. We were able to support everything from all sides via our strong volunteer networks. One is in a feminist utopia...Because these enable women to rebuild their lives and even survive, especially in Turkey where parental violence often replaces that of husbands after divorce and separation. Feminism was the thing reviving them, giving them hope and vitality."

Furthermore, Participant 3's experiences at the Purple Roof demonstrate the reciprocal nature of empowerment. Witnessing the women's resilience and their connection to feminism was empowering for her as well, highlighting the transformative power of feminist solidarity.

"It was incredible and very empowering for me. They were becoming so empowered that they all embraced and connected their experiences to feminism. As we all have done. This led to rapid changes in liberation, empowerment, and a zero-tolerance stance on violence. Witnessing their transformations in one or two years was very empowering..."

Feminist Initiatives within the Mainstream Community

As mentioned, in Turkey many of the psychoanalysts and psychoanalytically oriented practitioners operate in a rather mainstream fashion. Integrating feminist approaches into psychoanalytically oriented practice often requires challenging traditional therapist-client boundaries and risking criticism from colleagues. Yet, since consolidating her identity as a feminist psychologist, Participant 3 has been resorting to such feminist initiatives for the benefit of her clients.

"Even though I knew I might face criticism from the mainstream community, I also implemented strategies to loosen the rigidity of the analytic framework in order to incorporate feminist perspectives. There was a time when I provided practical information or attended court on behalf of a private client..."

It is also noteworthy that in those endeavors, Participant 3 specifically draws on her prior experiences at the Purple Roof. Convinced of their value, she dares to integrate such principles.

"At another instance, derived from my experience at the Purple Roof, I told a divorced client who was feeling weak and helpless after experiencing severe violence that she was actually very strong and competent in securing her and her children's safety, and her children had witnessed her powerful struggle... My supervisor commented that I violated psychoanalytic principles by stressing clients' power as she specifically brought her weaknesses to be addressed, a theme we disagreed on and discussed. This could have been received negatively by the professional community as well. By acknowledging her weak side but also emphasizing her strength, my remark was successful in empowering her and prompting her to declare that she was capable of surviving and taking care of her children."

Participant 3 insists on proceeding with these maneuvers despite the potential negative reactions from the professional environment. She stresses the success of her feminist strategies and persists in maintaining her ambivalent position in the eyes of the mainstream community. The below quote justifies her position.

> "We contain vulnerability. But I sincerely believe that it is crucial for us to recognize that we are rightful, powerful, and combative in the face of patriarchy. I still emphasize clients' power in my therapies, which does not correspond with mainstream psychoanalytical treatment. Mainstream psychoanalysis tends to constrain feminist work like this. I discuss such issues with my supervisor."

In summary, Participant 3's compelling story encapsulates contradictions, trajectories of suffering, and ambivalences in childhood and as a married woman, all of which contribute to solidifying her feminist consciousness. She reveals how incorporating feminist insights and maneuvers is a delicate dance vis-à-vis the orthodoxy prevailing in psychoanalytic communities. However, the effectiveness of her actions is a clear indicator of the necessity for mainstream approaches to incorporate feminist and critical perspectives in order to address the pervasive patriarchal violence in Turkey.

Participant 4: From Rejection to Rediscovering Psychology and Psychoanalysis

Participant 4 recounts a story of initially being skeptical and rejecting psychology as a means of social control, which gradually evolves into a transformative rediscovery of psychology and psychoanalysis that holds the potential to understand and challenge the patriarchal norms that engulf women's lives. Participant 4 presents a story that is made up of winding paths and circuitous trajectories, ultimately culminating in her use of psychoanalysis and feminism to reconnect with her own story. When asked by the researcher if she wanted to do the same for other women through psychoanalytically oriented feminist therapy, she responded positively.

Early Phase of Total Rejection of Psychology

Participant 4 begins her story from her undergraduate years when she had no idea about feminist psychology or feminism. In the meantime, as part of her process of politicizing, she endorses strong criticisms against psychology as a tool of authority and social control, which amount to a nihilist rejection. In her words, she now recognizes that her initial rejection of psychology was perhaps immature and uninformed.

> "We have nothing to gain; these departments have nothing to offer. These were my thoughts. We did not have a single discussion on feminist psychology, nor did we have a course on the topic…"

As a general phenomenon in Turkey, she describes the positivist cognitive-behaviorist school of thought offered at her department as "inadequate, lacking depth, irrelevant to social realities, uncritical, superficial, and weak in terms of theory and application." However, this rejection marked the beginning of a transformative journey. This journey was closely intertwined with her personal growth and self-discovery.

Discovering Feminism as a Decoder of Life and Entering Feminist Politics

After graduation, Participant 4 works as a counseling teacher at high schools where she witnesses numerous cases of gender-based violence amongst adolescents, which initially alerts her to the extensive nature of patriarchy and the need to turn to feminist understandings to counteract it.

> "I think my long-time work at high schools was influential… Oppressive relations among families, particularly towards adolescents, especially girls… Domestic violence, incest, dating violence, and digital violence…The adolescents were so unaware, just as we had been in our own days… I organized several trainings on patriarchal codes and the normalization of violence in romantic relationships…"

Her personal experiences as a woman, combined with her involvement in socialist political formations, led Participant 4 to recognize the sexist biases within her previous political affiliations and the importance of incorporating feminist principles into all forms of activism.

> "Gradually, I encountered feminism… Before, my political stance was more socialist. It is related to our own experiences of womanhood. Indeed, patriarchy is more than just a theory; it is deeply ingrained in life and permeates life experiences. In terms of politics, I came to realize how a feminist agenda is immensely important in any political mobilization. It also had to do with what I had experienced in these socialist organizations. Ignoring the presence and efforts of women, one cannot achieve a comprehensive political agenda while engaging in discrimination."

In her private life, her encounter with feminism enabled her to recognize injustices in her experiences that she had previously overlooked, prompting her to rename, reconsider, and reinterpret her own story to fully understand what she had truly undergone.

> "Over time, one often experiences patriarchy in emotional and social relationships. In my first emotional relationship, I had little awareness of manipulation, psychological violence, distorted perceptions, and gaslighting. Encountering feminism and feminist theory, one asks oneself what one has actually gone through. By decoding these, one can reinterpret and rewrite her story."

Participant 4 progressively increases her overall feminist consciousness by actively engaging with socialist feminist political mobilizations through various channels such as journals, trainings, meetings, and camps. Like all participants, she engages in TODAP, where her critical feminist reconnection with psychology occurs through interactions with a few feminist colleagues.

> "At TODAP, we, as feminist psychologists, have opened up a space that is nurturing both theoretically and practically through our gatherings, collective reflections, mutual learning, and collective attendance at the 8th of March marches. These greatly contributed to my re-reading, re-contacting, and reappropriation of psychological knowledge."

Additionally, she becomes affiliated with the Yogurtcu Women's Forum, which was formed after the anti-government Gezi uprisings in 2013. Here, she engages in weekly feminist discussions on various topics. Moreover, she organizes a 5-week series on feminist psychology with her colleagues. Thus, she takes on an active role in the dissemination and practice of feminist psychological knowledge.

> "These arenas, and of course my later work at the Purple Roof, were like circles within circles, corresponding to and integrating with my pursuits and contributing to me, just as I did to them. This evolution proceeded from rejection, to political struggle, then to feminist struggle, and culminated with my reencounter with psychology."

Reconnecting with Psychoanalysis while Reconnecting with the Self

In parallel and in interaction with the abovementioned processes, Participant 4 decides to go through psychoanalytic psychotherapy. She specifically seeks a clinician who is a feminist. After years of intense engagement with external realities and political activism, Participant 4 realizes that she had neglected her inner world, which she describes as having "congested spots". During this phase, her psychoanalytic journey gradually leads her to lean towards becoming a psychoanalytically oriented therapist herself.

"Turning inwards, I got to know psychoanalysis: its implementation and its experience. Reading about it also led me to explore it from a feminist perspective... These were phases of reflection and inner integration, leading me to decide to become a psychoanalytically oriented therapist..."

This process was fraught for Participant 4, with critical scrutiny of the patriarchal notions in classical theory as well. She regards the psychoanalysis cultivated by feminist contributions as an ally in contesting patriarchal mindsets.

"I also questioned classical psychoanalysis as a realm dominated by fathers and theories of male thinkers emphasizing sexuality and the phallus. Its outlook is also oppressive to LGBT people. Feminist theory has made significant contributions to the understanding of the female Oedipal process. With critical currents like feminism, psychoanalytic theory has evolved to explore the deepest dynamics of the human psyche, embracing everyone's dark sides and unique unconscious internal conflicts in a nonjudgmental manner."

This process of critical engagement with psychoanalysis was intertwined with personal pursuits and transformations.

"In fact, psychoanalytic theory as developed by feminism seems to me to be at odds with and rejects patriarchal codes. Maybe this is the reason I feel so close. Due to the fact that, during my journey, I had conflicts regarding psychoanalysis, and I gradually integrated them and underwent psychoanalysis myself..."

Nonetheless, Participant 4 is wary of patriarchal interpretations and harmful misapplications of psychoanalysis that are possible and prevalent, revealing her conclusive disavowal of them.

"Of course, there are many mainstream, conservative, and judgmental places and people, as well as a prevalence of homophobic colleagues. There are many mainstream places that operate in judgmental and reductionist ways... In our culture, there are even places that exalt motherhood and impose patriarchal views on women's sexuality. It was a journey: I mean my pursuits and my distancing myself from such people and institutions. I believe one cannot support a person by imposing a so-called 'conservative truth.' How can a clinician work with clients' defenses within prohibitions while rejecting the female body and sexuality, rendering them practically unspeakable or criminal?"

Starting as a personal journey for Participant 4, psychoanalytic work infused with feminism has evolved into an ideal of supporting women in reconnecting with their authentic selves by assisting them in decoding and challenging patriarchal realities in their lives, as she has done. To fulfill this ideal, soon after becoming a therapist, she decides to volunteer at the Purple Roof.

Becoming a Feminist Psychologist in Turkey

Purple Roof as an Arena for Activism, Multilateral Solidarity, and Practicing Feminist Psychology

Soon after embracing her identity as a psychoanalytically oriented feminist therapist, Participant 4 decides to volunteer at the Purple Roof, viewing it as a form of activism. This indicates how, like other participants, she does not neatly separate her identity as a clinician from her identity as a feminist activist.

> "I intended to do volunteer work at the Purple Roof shortly after deciding to become a therapist. There, I applied feminist psychology by uniting theory and practice in a practical manner. Before making my decision, I questioned and framed it as an act of activism and a contribution to feminist politics. Amid the solidarity present, my profession became intertwined with the feminist politics there. I considered and interpreted it as feminist politics and as women's solidarity."

However, women's solidarity is not just a one-way contribution from volunteers to resident women. Participant 4 points out that it actually entails multidirectional learning and empowerment experiences for all individuals involved.

> "Taking care of and doing inner work with women also improves me and makes me feel good. We are getting stronger together. Processing their stories together, thinking about each one individually. Women are not only victims; they are also very powerful agents. Despite these extremely difficult conditions, a lifelong immersion in patriarchal codes, economic pressures, and psychological strains...While women's mothers, fathers, and social circles may dictate that they remain in those cycles of violence, their struggles to break free and build their lives have taught me a lot."

Participant 4 also found it instructive to recognize the commonalities among workers, volunteers, and residents, pointing out the entrenchment and universality of patriarchy. This fact also cultivates Participant 4's beliefs in the righteousness and meaningfulness of their solidarity and this solidarity's function as feminist politics.

> "Women who would otherwise never have the chance to go to therapy, who come from different socio-economic segments and ages, including migrant women and women from diverse geographies and cultures. There are women from very traditional family codes, yet we see our similarities within the patriarchal system - similar stories, entrapments, and congestions, despite such immense differences. This is very instructive, showing the legitimacy of our solidarity and struggle."

This political act is most powerfully carried out by women collectively exposing patriarchal violence, thus dismantling the veil of social and cultural invisibility and challenging its legitimacy.

"Through all of our stories, collective efforts, and mutual solidarity at the Purple Roof, we strive to break through the veil of violence's invisibility and unspeakability within the 'holy' family and society, exacerbated by government policies. Through our work and mutual solidarity, we make violence visible, showing that we are here and acknowledge what has happened and continues to happen to you, me, and us. We counter each other's solitude, as if no one and no world exists outside of the patriarchy - just us and the vast world, with a sense of panic about the prospect of stepping out. Purple Roof supports women in breaking free from this simulation and realizing their own power and ability to stand on their own. These advance our feminist politics and struggles."

For Participant 4, rediscovering feminist-informed psychology and psychoanalysis served as a tool to reread and reinterpret patriarchal elements incorporating violence in her story, ultimately leading her to do the same for other women. Like all other participants, she regards this work conducted both at the shelter and in her private practice as inseparable from broader solidarity and feminist politics. Moreover, like Participant 3, she presents an alternative definition of instructive, inspiring, and empowering solidarity as a multilateral practice that also extends from women who have experienced violence to service providers. Finally, Participant 4's story points to how feminist psychology and feminist psychoanalytically oriented clinical work are potent tools to challenge patriarchal norms and empower women.

Discussion

Feminist therapy originated from the consciousness-raising groups and has since expanded and been institutionalized alongside feminist psychology and activism (Evans et al., 2011). Centered on the key principles of analyzing women's distress within dynamics of power and powerlessness embedded in oppressive political and socio-cultural contexts, feminist therapy undermines intrapsychic explanations of "individual level pathology" and androcentric psychological theories of mental health and human development by locating pathology externally in the dominant culture, patriarchal, and other power structures impinging on intersecting social identities (Brown, 2018).

Solidly consolidating itself over the years and incorporating various techniques built on core feminist principles of egalitarianism and empowerment, feminist therapists have devised integrative models and programs for treatment and practice, as well as tools to operationalize feminist concepts in research, family therapies, and distinct schools of thought. Furthermore, they promulgated intersectional identity development models, conducted outcome research, developed theories based on women's experiences, established paradigms for therapy supervision, and focused on the assessment and integration of diversity. Expanded by intersectional, multicultural, and critical psychological approaches, they established codes of ethics, professional organizations, institutions, conferences, and journals (Brown, 2018).

In the absence of such considerable and extensive accumulation and institutionalization, this study describes the efforts of a few feminist psychologists in a less democratic context marked by a strong, multilevel patriarchy infiltrating state policies. Through interrogating their accounts of discovering feminist psychology and psychoanalytic feminism and embracing their identities as feminist psychologists, this study uncovered that despite the lack of formal and readily available academic and institutional affiliations, and being immersed in a predominantly mainstream educational and professional setting, these individuals have all, through different paths, arrived at a shared understanding and dedication to the essential principles of feminism and feminist therapy. The narratives thus underscore the limited yet vital presence of feminist psychology, psychoanalytic feminism and feminist psychoanalysis in Turkey, practiced tentatively by a small group of psychologist-activists, while highlighting the dominance of mainstream education and practice, often permeated by misogynist and sexist practices.

The participants' narratives mostly illustrate their initial and enduring dissatisfaction surrounding their mainstream undergraduate and master's educations. This dissatisfaction was compensated by their participation in political movements and the consolidation of their feminist identities, informed by their experiences of womanhood. Participant 1's progressive pursuit stemmed from discontent with her conventional education, training, and operations in the field. However, this journey often encountered ambiguity in terms of accessing feminist psychological knowledge and included self-doubts about how to apply it within mainstream professional circles. Yet, for Participant 2, this quest incorporated a more progressive consolidation of self-assuredness and rejection of the mainstream knowledge and practice. Based on her personal experiences of womanhood, Participant 3 gradually incorporated feminist perspectives into her therapist identity through engagement with feminism and feminist activism. Finally, Participant 4 straightforwardly rejected psychology early on in her career; however, she later reconstituted a renewed endorsement of psychology and psychoanalysis, incorporating critical perspectives. Although, as feminists, all of the participants strove to surpass their mainstream psychology education throughout their journeys before becoming affiliated with the Purple Roof (mainly via TODAP), their volunteering experiences there have decisively integrated feminism and therapeutic practice. For all participants, working or volunteering at the Purple Roof has been pivotal in both consolidating their identities as feminist psychologists and informing their further feminist clinical work in their private practice. Yet, beyond merely operating within the constraints of their roles as psychologists, their narratives reveal how they positioned and gave meaning to their endeavors as an integral part of holistic efforts of solidarity, activism, broader feminist struggle, and politics that were also empowering for them. Overall, their work highlights the need for a deeper problematization of the limited integration of feminist and critical perspectives into mainstream approaches. These approaches, originating in Western contexts, still continue to exert dominant influences worldwide. Yet Turkey's current gender regime signals the urgent need for the incorporation of feminist perspectives into clinical education and training as well as the improvement of feminist resources in general.

As the consolidation of international feminist psychology is presented as a key agenda today, this study also highlights the importance of establishing international solidarities and connections, particularly with vulnerable countries where antifeminism and hostile gender politics are on the rise. As antigender politics fostered by authoritarian regimes, institutional transformations, and the overt elimination of women's rights escalate in many parts of the world as a historical co-construction, feminist psychologists can greatly benefit from transnational solidarity, connections, and knowledge as important actors in broader feminist politics. The challenges faced by feminist psychologists in Turkey might resonate with similar struggles in other contexts, highlighting the potential of transnational solidarity to address these challenges.

Acknowledgements

The author wants to thank Dr. Paul Sebastian Ruppel for his suggestions during data analysis, Dr. Pradeep Chakkarath, and Prof. Dr. Jürgen Straub for their support.

Funding

This project was funded by The International Psychoanalytic University (IPU) and the Hans Kilian and Lotte Köhler Center (KKC) for Social and Cultural Psychology and Historical Anthropology at Ruhr University Bochum, as part of the 2023-2024 Postdoctoral Fellowship for Social and Cultural Psychology and Psychoanalysis.

References

Acar, G., & Şah, D. (1990). Psychology in Turkey. *Psychology Developing Societies, 2*(2), 241-256.
Açikel, F., & Ateş, K. (2011). Ambivalent citizens: The Alevi as 'the authentic self' and the 'stigmatized other' of Turkish nationalism. *European Societies, 13*(5), 713–733.
Akadli-Ergocmen, B., Yuksel-Kaptanoglu, I., & Jansen, H. (2013). Intimate partner violence and the relation between help-seeking behavior and the severity and frequency of physical violence among women in Turkey. *Violence Against Women, 19*(9), 1151–1174.
Alan, H., Dereli-Yilmaz, S., Filiz, E., & Arioz, A. (2016). Domestic violence awareness and prevention among married women in central Anatolia. *Journal of Family Violence, 31*(6), 711–719.
Arat, Y. (1994). Women's movement of the 1980s in Turkey: Radical outcome of liberal Kemalism? In F. M. Göçek and B. Shiva (Eds.), *Reconstructing gender in the Middle East: Tradition, identity and power.* (pp. 100–112). New York: Columbia University Press.
Arat, Y. (2008). Contestation and collaboration: Women's struggles for empowerment in Turkey. In R Kasaba (Ed.), *The Cambridge history of Turkey: Turkey in the Modern World* (Vol 4., pp. 388-418). Cambridge: Cambridge University Press.
Arat, Y. (2023). The feminist movement in Turkey and the women of the Gezi Park protests. In C. Eschle & A. Bartlett (Eds.), *Feminism and protest camps* (pp. 99-114). Bristol University Press.
Aslıtürk, E., & Batur, S. (2014). Teknisyenlik ve toplumsallık arasında psikolojinin dünü, bugünü ve yarını. [The past, present and future of psychology between technician and sociality] *Eleştirel Psikoloji Bülteni, 5*, 1-17.
Baraitser, L. (2019). Psychoanalytic feminism. In Y. Stavrakakis (Ed.) *Routledge handbook of psychoanalytic political theory* (pp. 107-121). Routledge.
Benjamin, J. (1998). *Shadow of the other: Intersubjectivity and gender in psychoanalysis.* New York: Routledge.
Beckman, L. J. (2014). Training in feminist research methodology: Doing research on the margins. *Women & Therapy, 37*(1-2),164-177. https://doi.org/10.1080/02703149.2014.850347
Bora, A., & Günal, A. (2002). *90' larda Türkiye'de Feminizm* [Feminism in Turkey in the 90s]. İletişim Yayınları.
Bora, A., & Üstün, İ. (2005). *Sıcak aile ortamı: Demokratikleşme sürecinde kadın ve erkekler.* [Warm family atmosphere: Women and men in the democratization process]. TESEV Yayınları.
Boratav, H. B. (2011). Searching for feminism in psychology in Turkey. In A. Rutherford, R. Capdevila, V. Undurti, & I. Palmary, (Eds.), *Handbook of international feminisms: Perspectives on psychology, women, culture, and rights* (pp. 17-36). Springer New York. https://doi.org/10.1007/978-1-4419-9869-9_2
Brown, L. S. (2017). Contributions of feminist and critical psychologies to trauma psychology. In S. N. Gold (Ed.), *APA handbook of trauma psychology: Foundations in knowledge* (pp. 501-526). American Psychological Association. https://doi.org/10.1037/0000019-025

Brown, L. S. (2018). *Feminist therapy* (2nd ed.). American Psychological Association. https://doi.org/10.1037/0000092-000..
Chesler, P. (2018). *Women and madness*. Chicago Review Press.
Cohen, J. A., Kassan, A., Wada, K., & Suehn, M. (2022). The personal and the political: How a feminist standpoint theory epistemology guided an interpretative phenomenological analysis. *Qualitative Research in Psychology, 19*(4), 917-948.
Çağatay, S. (2019). Varieties of anti-gender mobilizations: Is Turkey a case? *LSE Engenderings, 9*. https://blogs.lse.ac.uk/gender/2019/01/09/varieties-of-anti-gender-mobilizations-is-turkey-a-case/
Çakır, S. (1994). *Osmanlı kadın hareketi* (Vol. 4). [*Ottoman women's movement*] İstanbul: Metis Yayınları.
Diner, Ç., & Tokaş, Ş. (2010). Waves of feminism in Turkey: Kemalist, Islamist and Kurdish women's movements in an era of globalization. *Journal of Balkan and Near Eastern Studies, 12*(1), 41-57.
Eichenbaum, L., & Obach, S. (2003). Relational psychoanalysis and feminism: a crossing of historical paths. *Psychotherapy and politics international, 1*(1), 17-26.
Ekal, B. (2017). Collaboration gone awry: The formation of women's shelters as public institutions in Turkey. *Mediterranean Politics, 24*(3), 320–337.
Evans, K. M., Kincade, E. A., & Seem, S. R. (2011). *Introduction to feminist therapy: Strategies for social and individual change*. Sage.
Fişek, G. O. (1990). Cinsiyet konumu ve psikoloji: Eleştirel bir inceleme [Gender position and psychology: A critical review [*Gender position and psychology: A critical review*]. *Toplum ve Bilim*, 50, 73-84.
Friedan, B. (1963). *The feminine mystique*. New York: W. W. Norton.
Gülerce, A. (2008). On the absence of a presence/the presence of an absence: Psychoanalysis in the Turkish context. *Theory & Psychology, 18*(2), 237-251.
Güneri, F. Y. (1996). Ailede kadına yönelik şiddet, evdeki terör, kadına yönelik şiddet. [Violence against women in the family, terror at home, violence against women] *İstanbul: Mor Çatı Yayınları*.
Herman, J. L. (2015). *Trauma and recovery: The aftermath of violence--from domestic abuse to political terror*. Hachette UK.
İlkkaracan, İ., & İlkkaracan, P. (1998). *Kuldan yurttaşa: Kadınlar neresinde?* [*From servant to citizen: Where are the women?*]. İstanbul: Türkiye Ekonomik ve Toplumsal Tarih Vakfı.
Irigaray, L. (1985). Speculum of the other woman (C. G. Gill, Trans.), New York: Cornell University Press. (Original work published 1974)
Kara, H., Ekici, A., & Inankul, H. (2014). The role of police in preventing and combating domestic violence in Turkey. *European Scientific Journal, 10*(20), 1-21.
Kamber, N. K. (2016). Feminism and psychoanalysis. In N. A. Naples, R. C. Hoogland, M. Wickramsinghe, W. C. A. Wong (Eds.) *The Wiley Blackwell encyclopedia of gender and sexuality studies* (pp. 1-10). Hoboken, New Jersey: Wiley-Blackwell.
Kayaoğlu, A., & Batur, S. (2013). Critical psychology in Turkey: Recent developments. *Annual Review of Critical Psychology, 10*, 916-931.
Kristeva, J. (1987) 'Freud and love: Treatment and its discontents'. *Tales of Love*. New York: Columbia University Press.
Maccoby, E. E., & Jacklin, C. N. (1974). *The Psychology of Sex Differences*. Stanford: Stanford University Press.

Marecek, J., & Hare-Mustin, R. T. (1991). A short history of the future: Feminism and clinical psychology. *Psychology of Women Quarterly, 15*(4), 521-536.
Marecek, J. (1995). Psychology and feminism: Can this relationship be saved?. In D. C. Stanton, & A. J. Stewart (Eds.) *Feminisms in the academy* (pp. 101-134). University of Michigan Press. https://works.swarthmore.edu/fac-psychology/1036
Mitchell, J. (1974). *Psychoanalysis and feminism: Freud, Reich, Laing, and Women.* New York: Vintage.
Pietkiewicz, I. & Smith, J. A. (2014). A practical guide to using interpretative . analysis in qualitative research psychology. *Psychological Journal, 20*(1), 7-14.
Sümer, N. (2016). Rapid growth of psychology programs in Turkey: Undergraduate curriculum and structural challenges. *Teaching of Psychology, 43*(1), 63-69.
Sunar, D., & Fisek, G. (2005). Contemporary Turkish families. In U. Gielen &J. Roopnarine (Eds.), *Families in global perspective* (pp. 169-183). Allyn & Bacon/Pearson.
Toktas, S., & Diner, C. (2015). Shelters for women survivors of domestic violence: A view from Turkey. *Women's Studies, 44*(5), 611–634.
Ussher, J. M. (2019). A critical feminist analysis of madness: Pathologising femininity through psychiatric discourse. In B. Cohen (Ed.) *Routledge international handbook of critical mental health* (pp. 72-78). Routledge.
We Will Stop Femicides Platform (n.d.). Veriler [Data]. https://kadincinayetlerinidurduracagiz.net/kategori/veriler
Yalcinoz-Ucan, B. (2022). Seeking safety from male partner violence in Turkey: Toward a context-informed perspective on women's decisions and actions. *Feminism & Psychology, 32*(4), 501-519.
Yılmaz, S. (2020). Çağdaş sivil toplum anlayışı yaklaşımıyla Mor Çatı Kadın Sığınağı Vakfı [Purple Roof Women's Shelter Foundation with its contemporary civil society approach]. *Bilgi Sosyal Bilimler Dergisi, 22*(2), 137-165.
Yüksel, S. (1995). A comparison of violent and non-violent families. In Ş. Tekeli Ed.). *Women in modern Turkish society: A reader* (pp. 275-287). London: Zed Books.

Doing Research on Feminism, Activism and Social Change for Gender Equality: Reflections of a Researcher from Turkey

Özden Melis Uluğ

University of Sussex, School of Psychology, Falmer, United Kingdom

Researchers have long been interested in studying gender inequality, injustice and discrimination in social sciences. Even though social psychology as a field has also investigated gender inequality (Brandt, 2011) and how women, as disadvantaged group members, challenge it (Kelly & Breinlinger, 1995), less attention has been given to these problems and the actions taking place against these problems in relatively challenging and less democratic contexts, such as Turkey. In these contexts, it is crucial to understand how, why, and when collective action for gender equality occurs, as the factors that affect activism in such contexts may differ from those in relatively more democratic ones (Uluğ et al., 2022). In this chapter, I aim to tackle this question—why women take action for gender equality in such contexts—and discuss how tackling this question, as well as my own collective action experiences in Turkey, has shaped my research(er) and feminist identity.

In addition to disadvantaged groups' action motivations for their own groups, recent research has also focused on actions taken by disadvantaged groups for other disadvantaged groups (e.g., inter-minority solidarity; see also Burson & Godfrey, 2020; Glasford & Calcagno, 2012). Facing discrimination due to being a disadvantaged or minority group member may help people perceive commonalities among different types of discrimination and support the coalition of their group with other minority groups (Craig & Richeson, 2016). For instance, Craig and Richeson (2012) showed that perceived discrimination against Latinos affects Latinos' attitudes toward Blacks by activating a common ingroup identity, such as a disadvantaged racial minority group identity (see also Chayinska et al., 2025). Similarly, it has been shown that discrimination experiences of different minority groups (e.g., feminists, LGBTQ+, Kurds) create cooperation among these groups to work against a shared goal (Acar & Uluğ, 2016). In my own research, I also worked on how women in general, but feminist women in particular, stand in solidarity with other disadvantaged groups in Turkey. In this chapter, I also aim to understand the solidarity dynamics between women and LGBTQ+s.

Focusing on these topics, constantly reflecting on my identities, and collecting data from disadvantaged groups in authoritarian contexts have helped me identify the research challenges. In this chapter, therefore, I aim to discuss the conceptual (e.g., multiplicity of identities), methodological (e.g., lack of mixed-method studies), and contextual challenges (e.g., insufficient emphasis on structural and political contexts) for feminist researchers in studying collective action (see also Uluğ et al., 2022 for challenges related to collective action research in general). Before presenting my research and its associated challenges, I first provide my positionality statement.

The Personal is Political: Intersecting Feminist, Activist, and Researcher Identities

"The personal is political" is a phrase coined by Carol Hanisch during the second-wave feminist movement in the 1970s, challenging the public and private divide (Lee, 2007). The third-wave feminism movement has reinterpreted the phrase (Schuster, 2017) and emphasized the importance of everyday feminism in challenging gender inequality through individual actions without necessarily involving themselves in collective efforts (Kelly, 2015). I argue that using research as a feminist tool to challenge gender inequality can also be seen as an individual act of everyday feminism.

I am a researcher in social psychology who identifies as a feminist and (former) activist. I argue that my feminist and activist identities shape my researcher identity, the way I conduct research, the methodologies I use, and the topics I choose to study (e.g., Uluğ et al., 2020, 2021). I came to the realization of this when I started collecting data from feminist women right after the Gezi Park protests.[1] This realization became a milestone in my life as a researcher because when I was an undergraduate student in psychology at the Middle East Technical University (METU) in Turkey, I was often told that I needed to be *objective* as a psychology researcher. The main narrative in psychology as a discipline relies on the assumption that "psychological science is objective, generalizable, and value free (or neutral)" (Breen & Darlaston-Jones, 2010, p. 67). I had internalized this assumption when I started my PhD in 2011. However, using different methods of epistemologies (e.g., qualitative methods;

---

1   The Gezi Park protests began in May 2013 in Istanbul to oppose the planned destruction of Gezi Park, one of the city's few remaining green spaces, and quickly expanded into a broader movement against the ruling AKP government. Initially started by environmental activists, the protests grew to include over three million participants across 79 cities, advocating for diverse causes like constitutional changes and greater freedom of expression.

Uluğ et al., 2017) and conducting research in various contexts (e.g., Germany; Odağ et al., 2023) with different groups (e.g., activists; Selvanathan et al., 2023) has challenged this assumption of mine.

More importantly, participating in the Gezi Park protests was a transformational experience for me in terms of having close contact with feminists and hearing their voices and concerns closely. I also noticed during the demonstrations that I felt very close to the women who raised these concerns (e.g., "avoid sexist chanting"). This experience itself helped me start asking myself questions such as, 'Why do I not call myself a feminist?', 'Why do I avoid the term?' and 'Why do I not want to be associated with feminists?' After this experience, I started reading more about feminism (e.g., Full Frontal Feminism by Jessica Valenti) and gender inequality (e.g., feminism is for everyone by bell hooks). This critical reflection process enabled me to interrogate the stigma surrounding the term "feminist," fostering a deeper understanding of its complexities. Additionally, it facilitated my identification with fellow feminists and my understanding of why women generally avoid the term.

In the following years, I became more active in women's rights campaigns and started calling myself an activist as well. In 2015, I saw an ad on Facebook for a tea brand (Doğadan) in which a man asked, "What do women want?" answering himself hastily using a long list of stereotypically female attributes (e.g., high-heel shoes with unbroken heels, an ideal body, pastries without gaining weight). As the ad was the embodiment of sexism, I wanted to take action against it. I created a Change.org petition and began sharing it on various social media platforms. Over 20,000 people signed the petition against the sexist ad in three days. This whole process ended with a halt to the advertisement. A public apology by the company, Doğadan, and the ad agency, Plasenta, to the protesting people followed. Later, Change.org asked me to prepare a video to thank all the campaign supporters.[2] During this process, I became quite active in women's rights activism.

When My Feminist and Researcher Identity Overlap: Studying Why Women Take Action

While I was working on my own to conduct my Change.org campaign, the founder of Erktolia.org—a pro-active platform that exposes and takes action against everyday sexism in Turkey—contacted me and asked if I could join them in the fight against sexism. I immediately joined this platform, started working as the Director of Communications, and continued in this role until

---

2 Please see the video on YouTube: https://www.youtube.com/watch?v=D3c_M5qpu3k

June 2017. On this platform, I was responsible for communicating with companies, organizations, and their employees to convince them to change their sexist (and transphobic) language in their online and offline statements, ads, and social media postings. I prepared and edited response letters to those companies and I had to be extra careful to avoid sexist language and to be more inclusive. Between April 2015 and June 2017, I monitored social media platforms such as Facebook, Twitter, and Instagram in general, as well as the online content of company websites, in particular, to expose sexism on those platforms and take necessary action. All of these experiences also made me much more aware of how sexism permeates various aspects of society and influences perceptions and interactions in everyday life. This heightened awareness has driven me to actively advocate for gender equality, challenge discriminatory practices wherever I encounter them, and use my own research to do that.

My online activism experience has also motivated me to ask some research questions. For example, I was intrigued by the question of why people in general, but women in particular, supported this online Doğadan campaign I conducted. This is how I merged my feminist activist identity with my research identity for the first time. I decided to conduct a study together with my colleagues, Özen Odağ and Nevin Solak, and we examined women's willingness to engage in similar collective action for gender justice in the future. As I had worked closely with Change.org (Turkey branch) during my Doğadan campaign, I contacted them and asked whether collaboration was possible to understand campaign supporters' motivations. They accepted my offer, and we started the collaboration together.

In the study (Uluğ et al., 2020), we aimed to investigate protest motivations behind the Doğadan case by looking at the influence of (a) online and offline collective action practices and (b) the three social-psychological variables of collective action (i.e., just world beliefs, social identity, and perceived efficacy). These three predictors have been suggested as part of the Social Identity Model of Collective Action (SIMCA; van Zomeren et al., 2008). We had three hypotheses: (1) Both offline (conceptualized as *liking to express opinions on the streets*) and online (conceptualized as *liking to express opinions on social media*) collective action practices would predict people's willingness to engage in collective actions against sexism. (2) Willingness to engage in collective actions against sexism would be predicted by social identity (conceptualized as *women's rights defender identity*), perceived efficacy (conceptualized as *the perceived efficacy of women's rights defenders*), as well as perceived injustice (conceptualized as *the rejection of just world beliefs*). (3) Three social-psychological variables would predict collective action intentions, even when controlling for participants' online/offline protest practices as well as their demographic characteristics (e.g., gender, age, and education).

We collected data from 353 participants who signed the Doğadan online petition to test these hypotheses.

The results highlighted that people's offline and online collective action practices would predict their future collective action intentions against sexism (confirming the first hypothesis). The results also showed that people's willingness to engage in collective action was predicted by stronger women's rights defender identification and perceived efficacy as well as weaker beliefs in a just world (confirming the second hypothesis). The three SIMCA predictors predicted willingness to engage in collective action against sexism even when controlling for people's online and offline collective action practices and their demographic variables characteristics (Uluğ et al., 2020). Thus, the results also confirmed the third hypothesis.

What do these results mean for gender rights and collective action in Turkey? We argued that in the Doğadan case, petitioning on Change.org was considered an efficient means, perhaps because of the inconspicuousness of the topic: a tea advert. However, one can also argue that people's choices may be quite different if they want to protest something that is more closely related to Erdoğan's misogynist politics (Özcan, 2018). Our research indicates that the social-psychological factors shown in the SIMCA—perceived injustice, efficacy, and identity—are crucial predictors of change in Turkey's current authoritarian environment, surpassing the influence of online and offline actions alone.

As mentioned earlier, I also conducted another study with the activists who participated in the Gezi Park protests (Uluğ & Acar, 2014, 2015; see also Acar & Uluğ, 2014, 2015). In this study, we aimed to examine social activism and identity constructs from a social psychological perspective to better understand the structure of the Gezi Park protests, the participants, and how they negotiated identities. Even though my colleague, Yasemin Gülsüm Acar, and I collected data from various ethnic, religious, and political groups (e.g., Alevi activists and anti-capitalist Muslims; $N = 34$), we also interviewed feminists and asked why they participated in the Gezi Park protests ($n = 3$). Feminist women mentioned various reasons for their participation, such as a reaction to the government's policies, a ban on abortion and morning-after pills, violence against women, and a lack of resources for battered women. Other reasons also included the unemployment problem of women, being in danger of losing freedom, not having a place on the street, having no say in politics, and being forced to have at least three children. All of these reasons show that women have different yet overlapping motivations for taking action towards gender equality, even when participating in a larger protest such as the Gezi Park protests.

My interaction with feminist activists in this study affected my way of thinking as a researcher and, thus, my future studies. For example, when I interviewed feminist women, all of them showed me that gender inequality is such a deeply rooted and multifaceted issue, intertwining with cultural, economic, and political factors that make it incredibly complex to address and fully understand. Yet, these women chose activism and decided to fight against gender inequality, patriarchy, and misogyny. This realization also made me want to conduct more studies with women in general, and feminist women in particular.

More recently, I conducted another study in Turkey to replicate the same study we conducted in Ukraine and the US in a different context and with a slightly different population. In this study, we examined the roles of (a) witnessing gender discrimination (conceptualized as *the frequency of having witnessed an incident of gender discrimination in day-to-day lives*) and (b) women-to-women support (conceptualized as *the support women receive from their social networks to take action to promote gender justice*) in women's willingness to engage in collective action for gender equality (Uluğ et al., 2023). We collected data from the general women population in Ukraine and the US. However, in Turkey, we chose feminists as a politicized woman's group for two reasons. First, the feminist movement in Turkey is strong even though the country's gender equality score is not that high (133rd largest gender gap among 156 countries; Global Gender Gap Report, 2021). Second, political actions are suppressed in the country, particularly following the 2016 coup attempt.[3] Yet feminists' actions are visible both offline and online (e.g., protests to support the Istanbul Convention[4]; Öztunç, 2023). In addition, we argued that women-to-women support and solidarity are high in this community, given the pressure women receive from the government and their close circles.

In this study (Uluğ et al., 2023), we collected data from a large sample of feminist women in Turkey ($N = 1304$). We investigated whether (1) witnessing incidents of gender discrimination among women predicts their willingness to engage in feminist collective action and (2) perceived women-to-women support moderates the relation between women's witnessing acts of gender discrimination and their willingness to engage in collective action for gender justice. We were particularly interested in this moderation hypothesis because, on the one hand, perceived social support can help people cope with the adverse effects of discrimination (e.g., Dennehy & Dasgupta, 2017; Mossakowski &

---

3 The 2016 coup attempt in Turkey took place on the night of July 15, 2016, when a faction within the Turkish military tried to overthrow the democratically elected government led by President Recep Tayyip Erdoğan. However, the attempt was not successful. It marked the beginning of a new chapter for Turkish politics, with Erdoğan emerging stronger and opposition voices facing increased repression (see also Uluğ & Acar, 2018).

4 The Istanbul Convention is a legally binding document to fight against all forms of violence against women (Güneş & Ezikoğlu, 2023). Even though Turkey was the first country to sign the agreement in 2011, it withdrew from it in 2021. The withdrawal itself sparked many protests in the country (Eski, 2021).

Zhang, 2014). On the other hand, perceived social support can encourage action to fight against discrimination (e.g., Gil de Zúñiga & Valenzuela, 2011; Son & Lin, 2008). Thus, women-to-women support can strengthen or weaken the link between witnessing gender discrimination and willingness to engage in collective action for gender justice.

The results showed that among self-identified feminist women in Turkey (1) witnessing gender discrimination significantly predicted women's willingness to engage in collective action for gender justice. In other words, the more women witnessed gender discrimination, the more willing they were to engage in collective action for gender justice. That was the case even after we controlled for women's personal experiences of gender discrimination (i.e., how often women themselves reported being a target of gender discrimination in their day-to-day lives). The results also highlighted that (2) perceived women-to-women support moderated the relationship between witnessing gender discrimination and willingness to take action for it within the same context and sample. Still, this relationship was stronger for women who reported having lower (vs. higher) women-to-women support in their lives. We should also note that our findings should not be interpreted as suggesting that perceived women-to-women support discourages women's willingness to act against gender discrimination. Instead, we demonstrate that while women-to-women support (whether low or high) encourages women to take action, the link between witnessing gender discrimination and willingness to participate in collective action for gender justice is more pronounced when this support is lower. Among feminists in Turkey, there may already be a high willingness to take action against gender discrimination. Yet, they can take action even more quickly when they do not see enough support from other women who are expected to advocate for gender equality.

Expanding the Solidarity Circle: Why Women Take Action for Marginalized Groups

Since I started identifying as a feminist and researching why women take action for gender equality, I have become more interested in intergroup solidarity and allyship not only as a concept (see, e.g., Uluğ et al., 2024) but also as a practice (see, e.g., Selvanathan et al., 2023). For me, being a feminist has meant not only fighting against gender inequality and discrimination but also standing in solidarity with other marginalized groups (see also Painia, 2018). That is why I also started researching how and why women engage in action for other disadvantaged groups (e.g., Tropp & Uluğ, 2019). For example, in one study we conducted in the US, we tried to understand white women's—who occupy an advantaged position on the basis of race and a disadvantaged position on the basis of gender (see McIntosh, 1988)—support for racial justice. We argued that white women's closeness with members of groups that have been targeted by prejudice may play a role in motivating them to take action for racial justice. We also hypothesized that white women's motivation and willingness to engage in protests for racial justice would be related not only to their close relationships with people who are targeted by prejudice, but also to the positive contact they have had with people of color (i.e., disadvantaged groups). To examine our hypotheses, we collected data from white women in the US across two studies ($N = 518$). We measured their intergroup contact (conceptualized as *the quality of their everyday intergroup contact experiences with people of color*), closeness to people targeted by prejudice (conceptualized as *the frequency of someone they care about being subject to public insults or slurs because of their race, ethnicity, or religion*), and willingness to engage and participation in protests for racial justice (conceptualized as *supporting the Black Lives Matter movement by being willing to participate/participating in various forms of actions such as protests, forums, or online actions*). The results showed that white women's positive interactions with people of color and their closeness to people targeted by prejudice predicted their willingness to engage in protests for racial justice. However, their actual participation (not just willingness) was predicted only by their closeness to people targeted by prejudice. These findings suggest that a certain level of awareness of inequality or unequal treatment (e.g., being aware of how disadvantaged groups are treated in public) might be required for those in privileged positions to take proactive steps toward becoming allies (see also Uluğ & Tropp, 2021).

In addition to exploring the question of how and why women take action for other disadvantaged groups in the US, I was also interested in studying this question in my own country, with the group I identify with: feminist women in Turkey. We have recently conducted three studies ($N = 1065$) and collected data from heterosexual feminist women to understand their motivations for participating in solidarity-based collective action for LGBTQ+ rights (Uysal et al., 2022). We particularly focused on heterosexual feminist women's solidarity because we wanted to use an intersectional approach. This group has an advantaged identity based on their sexual orientation (heterosexual), a disadvantaged identity based on their gender (woman), and a politicized identity based on their ideological position (feminist). We hypothesized that (1) stronger feminist identification (conceptualized as *how being a feminist defines one's identity, fosters strong bonds and solidarity with other feminists, and highlights shared experiences*), (2) higher perceived discrimination against LGBTQ+ (conceptualized as *awareness of increasing hostility, intolerance, and threats toward the LGBTQ+ community*), and (3) greater endorsement of strategic intra-minority alliance between feminists and LGBTQ+ (conceptualized as *the belief that feminists and LGBTQ+ groups should collaborate to strengthen their positions and achieve shared goals*) would be linked with greater willingness to participate in solidarity-based collective action (conceptualized as *being willing to participate in various forms of actions such as protests, forums, or online actions for LGBTQ+ rights*).

The results showed that higher feminist identification (but not woman identification) consistently predicted feminists' willingness to participate in solidarity-based collective action for LGBTQ+ across three studies. However, more perceived discrimination against LGBTQ+ was not a consistent predictor of feminists' willingness to take action (significant relationship only in Study 2). Endorsement of strategic intra-minority alliance between feminists and LGBTQ+ predicted feminists' willingness to participate in solidarity-based collective action across all three studies. Based on these findings, we argue that women take action for other marginalized groups as long as their woman identity is politicized, they believe in intergroup solidarity, and are aware of marginalized groups' discrimination experiences and their own privileges based on their advantaged identities.

Feminist Researchers' Challenges in Studying (Collective Action for) Gender Equality

All these research experiences made me reflect on the challenges of researching gender inequality, collective action, and social change in difficult contexts like Turkey. These challenges include, but are not limited to (a) conceptual, (b) methodological, and (c) contextual challenges (see Uluğ et al., 2022, for a discussion of challenges in studying collective action). One of the first challenges I had was a conceptual challenge. Let's take a look at women's identity as a concept. Although many studies focus on women's identity (e.g., Kelly & Breinlinger, 1995) and its variations (e.g., women's rights defender identity; Uluğ et al., 2020) to understand their role in collective action for gender equality, as a researcher, we usually do not know what those identities mean for those participants and what the content of those identities looks like for them (see Mikołajczak et al., 2022). Women hold a variety of identities, each representing different meanings and experiences for them. These identities may sometimes even have opposite meanings for those who adopt traditional gender roles vs those who have feminist views (Becker & Wagner, 2009). It is challenging to focus on these various identities, understand their precursors, and unpack their role in motivating women's collective action tendencies when the same concepts may mean different things to women. This challenge is even more exacerbated when certain methodological approaches limit us, which brings me to the second challenge.

The second challenge I had was a methodological challenge. In traditional psychology, researchers commonly use scales, such as Likert scales, to quantify and measure various psychological phenomena, including attitudes, behaviors, and personality traits. These scales provide a structured way to assess individuals' responses and facilitate statistical analysis. By using scales, researchers can gather data that allows for comparisons and conclusions about psychological constructs in a reliable and valid manner. For example, in my own research, I use feminist identification or woman identification as these measures help me understand to extent to which women identify with these different identities.

Similarly, when approaching participants with a predefined set of variables, we usually cannot consider their multiple identities (see Uysal et al., 2022, for an exception). For example, when collecting data from Kurdish women in Turkey to understand why they take to the streets for women's rights, it is almost impossible to get a complete picture if we only focus on their woman identity, but not on their Kurdish identity. In many cases, a singular identity framework does not work due to the multiplicity of identities individuals have (Greenwood, 2012). In such cases, it may be helpful to allow participants to first define themselves and ask to what extent they identify with such identities, or ask open-ended questions to better understand their multiple identities. Therefore, more qualitative or mixed methods studies are needed to capture identity complexities and overcome some of these methodological challenges when studying gender and activism. Based on these qualitative and mixed-method findings, dimensions of woman identity can be better understood and expanded to include a more nuanced understanding of the roles, experiences, and social expectations that shape their sense of self, allowing for a broader appreciation of the diverse factors influencing woman identity and perceptions of that identity across different cultural, social, and personal contexts (see also Ciaffoni, 2024).

I also had some contextual challenges while conducting studies on these topics in Turkey, which is the third challenge. For example, I started collecting data from various marginalized groups (e.g., women, Kurds, Alevis, etc.) after the Gezi Park protests ended in 2013. Especially in 2014, Turkey's political atmosphere began to change. The attempted coup in the country in 2016 and the subsequent state of emergency marked a critical period in the country's modern history. The AKP government used this attempt to consolidate power and maintain its hold on the government (Acar & Uluğ, 2022). The state of emergency significantly curtailed civil liberties, leading to criticism from international human rights organizations accusing the government of using the coup as a pretext to crack down on political dissent. The political actions of the opposition have been suppressed harshly by the government as a result. Turkey is, therefore, categorized as a competitive authoritarian regime (Esen & Gumuscu, 2016; Levitsky & Way, 2002).

In one study we conducted, we tried to examine how different forms of collective action and voting as political tools and as a means to create viable change are perceived in authoritarian contexts (Uluğ et al., 2025). We collected data from opposition members ($N = 152$); however, almost two-thirds of the participants identified as women ($n = 95$). Therefore, I believe the findings highlight something important concerning women's understanding of collective action. In the study, we asked open-ended questions in an online survey (e.g., Some people attend street protests to make their voices heard in Turkey's current political environment. What do you think about participating in this kind of collective action [e.g., protest or attend a meeting] to make your voice heard regarding Turkey's current political environment?). We analyzed the data using qualitative content analysis. The results highlighted opposition members' diverse opinions on offline and online protests to make their voices heard. For example, in Turkey, offline protests are mainly seen as necessary, a right, and an effective political tool; however, they are also perceived as very dangerous and frightening. Despite higher costs associated with protests in Turkey (Anisin, 2016), some participants argue that offline protests are more impactful than voting to express opinions.

While *online* protests are considered useful yet potentially dangerous, concerns about their effectiveness deter some people from participating in social media activism (see Acar et al., 2024). These findings illustrate the varied perspectives on unconventional political participation in risky environments. Kentmen-Çin (2015) notes that traditional explanations of political action do not apply well in Turkey, where even low-risk online actions can lead to severe repercussions. Our research highlights how perceived costs and risks influence opposition members' views on the effectiveness of these actions, warranting further investigation (see also Uluğ et al., 2022). These findings also show that it is getting increasingly difficult to conduct studies on collective action, protests, and activism and ask marginalized groups questions about their involvement in such actions. Therefore, authoritarian contexts make it hard for researchers to study these topics in particular.

Concluding Remarks and Suggestions for Future Research

In this chapter, I aimed to reflect on my academic journey as a researcher from Turkey and explore the intersections of feminism, activism, and social change for gender equality. I discussed how my personal and activist identities have shaped my research journey by specifically discussing my experiences during the Gezi Park protests and my growing involvement in women's rights campaigns and activism.

Throughout my research, I have examined how and why women engage in actions not only for their own rights but also for other marginalized groups, such as LGBTQ+ communities. I reflected on the conceptual, methodological, and contextual challenges of conducting research on collective action concerning women's rights. Based on these experiences and reflections, I argued the benefits of intersectional approaches, the necessity of qualitative and mixed methods for a more nuanced approach as well as the potential limitations and opportunities authoritarian regimes create for researchers who work on women's rights and collective action for social change.

Further questions still need to be addressed concerning women's rights in Turkey. First, given that violence against women has increased in recent years, especially after the withdrawal from the Istanbul Convention, researchers should consider how women cope with the effects of both witnessing and experiencing everyday violence as well as how their coping mechanisms translate into (not) taking action for gender equality in Turkey. Similarly, researchers may focus on the role of women-to-women support in coping with the adverse effects of experiencing and witnessing everyday violence. Understanding these coping mechanisms can provide valuable insights into the resilience of women and the effectiveness of informal support networks, especially in authoritarian contexts. It may also inform the development of targeted interventions that empower women, enhance their agency, and foster collective action toward achieving gender equality.

Second, researchers should consider when the tipping point is for women to take action in authoritarian contexts like Turkey. As mentioned earlier, protests are often risky and costly in such contexts (Odağ et al., 2023). However, this does not prevent women from taking (further) action because repression in such contexts can also backfire and motivate people to challenge the repression itself (Ayanian et al., 2021; Ayanian & Tausch, 2016; see also Gezici-Yalçın & Uluğ, 2017). Recent demonstrations in October 2024 that took place for İkbal Uzuner ve Ayşenur Halil—two young women who a man, Semih Çelik, brutally killed—represent this type of resistance. One of the significant characteristics of these protests was that they also attracted men's support. For example, male students from İstanbul Boys' High School joined these protests (Temoçin, 2024). Therefore, it is also essential to understand the tipping points for advantaged groups (i.e., potential allies) to take solidarity-based actions for disadvantaged or marginalized groups. Future studies may investigate whether tipping points for advantaged groups differ from those for disadvantaged groups and compare them.

Third, future studies may focus on solidarity between feminist women and other disadvantaged and marginalized groups. For example, my studies only focused on the solidarity between feminists and LGBTQ+s in Turkey (e.g.,

Uysal et al., 2022), but did not focus on solidarity between feminists and other marginalized groups. Even though solidarity between the (Turkish) feminist movement and the Kurdish (feminist) movement has been studied in social sciences (e.g., Erengezgin, 2021; Küçükkırca, 2018), there has not been a social psychological approach to examine how, for example, intersectional awareness as a construct (Curtin et al., 2015) may play an important role in standing in solidarity with disadvantaged and activist groups among women in general, and feminist women in particular. More studies are needed to understand the (lack of) solidarity dynamics between feminists on the one hand and Alevis, Kurds, Armenians, and environmentalists on the other hand.

My journey as a researcher navigating the complexities of feminism, activism, and social change in Turkey has revealed how personal experiences shape collective actions toward gender equality and justice. The challenges highlighted in my research emphasize the necessity for a nuanced understanding of intersectionality and the vital role of solidarity among marginalized groups. As the political landscape shifts in the world (but particularly in authoritarian contexts), it becomes increasingly clear that individual identities and lived experiences are deeply interconnected with broader political currents. Ultimately, recognizing that 'personal is political' allows us to see that our individual experiences are not just personal struggles, but are part of a larger system that fuels collective action against it and drives societal change for gender equality. In this light, the personal becomes a catalyst for political transformation, empowering us all to partake in the ongoing fight for equality and justice through activism or research, and sometimes through both.

References

Acar, Y. G., & Uluğ, Ö. M. (2014). The body politicised: The visibility of women at Gezi. *ROAR Magazine*. http://roarmag.org/2014/01/women-gezi-park-protests/
Acar, Y. G., & Uluğ, Ö. M. (2015). "Becoming us without being one": A social psychological perspective on the Gezi Park protesters and negotiating levels of identity. In G. Koc & H. Aksu (Eds.), *Another brick in the barricade: The Gezi resistance and its aftermath* (pp. 34-54). Wiener Verlag für Sozialforschung.
Acar, Y. G., & Uluğ, Ö. M. (2016). Examining prejudice reduction through solidarity and togetherness experiences among Gezi Park activists in Turkey. *Journal of Social and Political Psychology*, 4(1), 166-179. https://doi.org/10.5964/jspp.v4i1.547
Acar, Y. G., & Uluğ, Ö. M. (2022). When and why does political trust predict well-being in authoritarian contexts? Examining the role of political efficacy and collective action among opposition voters. *British Journal of Social Psychology*, 61(3), 861-881. https://doi.org/10.1111/bjso.12505
Acar, Y. G., Uluğ, Ö. M., Solak, N., & Şen, E. (2024). Political resistance in Turkey: How resistance is experienced and how it has changed over the last decade. In F. B.

Zeineddine & J. R. Vollhardt (Eds.), *Resistance to repression and violence: Global psychological perspectives* (pp. 115-134). Oxford University Press. https://doi.org/10.1093/9780197687703.003.0006

Anisin, A. (2016). Repression, spontaneity, and collective action: The 2013 Turkish Gezi protests. *Journal of Civil Society, 12*(4), 411-429. https://doi.org/10.1080/17448689.2016.1239607

Ayanian, A. H., Tausch, N., Acar, Y. G., Chayinska, M., Cheung, W. Y., & Lukyanova, Y. (2021). Resistance in repressive contexts: A comprehensive test of psychological predictors. *Journal of Personality and Social Psychology, 120*(4), 912-939. https://doi.org/10.1037/pspi0000285

Ayanian, A. H., & Tausch, N. (2016). How risk perception shapes collective action intentions in repressive contexts: A study of Egyptian activists during the 2013 post-coup uprising. *British journal of social psychology, 55*(4), 700-721. https://doi.org/10.1111/bjso.12164

Becker, J. C., & Wagner, U. (2009). Doing gender differently: The interplay of strength of gender identification and content of gender identity in predicting women's endorsement of sexist beliefs. *European Journal of Social Psychology, 39*, 487-508. https://doi.org/10.1002/ejsp.551

Brandt, M. J. (2011). Sexism and gender inequality across 57 societies. *Psychological Science, 22*(11), 1413-1418. https://doi.org/10.1177/0956797611420445

Breen, L. J., & Darlaston-Jones, D. (2010). Moving beyond the enduring dominance of positivism in psychological research: Implications for psychology in Australia. *Australian Psychologist, 45*(1), 67-76. https://doi.org/10.1080/00050060903127481

Burson, E., & Godfrey, E. B. (2020). Intraminority solidarity: The role of critical consciousness. *European Journal of Social Psychology, 50*(6), 1362-1377. https://doi.org/10.1002/ejsp.2679

Chayinska, M., Uluğ, Ö. M., Woo, Y. T., Brik, T., & Caricati, L. (2025). Witnessing racial discrimination predicts intra-minority allyship but not through identification with all humanity. Manuscript submitted for publication.

Ciaffoni, S. (2024). *Through Medusa's gaze: exploring women's perception of gender inequalities and its relevance to social change* (Unpublished doctoral dissertation). University of Bologna.

Craig, M. A., & Richeson, J. A. (2012). Coalition or derogation? How perceived discrimination influences intra-minority intergroup relations. *Journal of Personality and Social Psychology, 102*(4), 759–777. https://doi.org/10.1037/a0026481

Craig, M. A., & Richeson, J. A. (2016). Stigma-based solidarity: Understanding the psychological foundations of conflict and coalition among members of different stigmatized groups. *Current Directions in Psychological Science, 25*(1), 21–27. https://doi.org/10.1177/0963721415611252

Curtin, N., Stewart, A. J., & Cole, E. R. (2015). Challenging the status quo: The role of intersectional awareness in activism for social change and pro-social intergroup attitudes. *Psychology of Women Quarterly, 39*(4), 512-529. https://doi.org/10.1177/0361684315580439

Dennehy, T. C., & Dasgupta, N. (2017). Female peer mentors early in college increase women's positive academic experiences and retention in engineering. *Proceedings of the National Academy of Sciences, 114*(23), 5964–5969. https://doi.org/10.1073/pnas.1613117114

Erengezgin, B. C. (2021). Coloniality and solidarity: an intersectional study of the relationship between the Turkish feminist movement and the Kurdish women's movement since the 1980s (Doctoral dissertation, University of British Columbia).
Esen, B., & Gumuscu, S. (2016). Rising competitive authoritarianism in Turkey. *Third World Quarterly, 37*(9), 1581-1606. https://doi.org/10.1080/01436597.2015.1135732
Eski, B. (2021). Protests as Turkey pulls out of treaty to protect women. The Guardian. https://www.theguardian.com/world/2021/mar/20/turkey-pulls-out-of-international-accord-designed-to-protect-women
Gezici-Yalçın, M., & Uluğ, Ö. M. (2017). "Gezi, bardağı taşıran son damlaydı": Sosyal psikolojik bir perspektifle Gezi Parkı isyanını anlamak ["Gezi was the last drop!": Understanding the Gezi Park protests from a social-psychological perspective]. *Türk Psikoloji Yazıları, 39*, 96-109.
Gil de Zúñiga, H., & Valenzuela, S. (2011). The mediating path to a stronger citizenship: Online and offline networks, weak ties, and civic engagement. *Communication Research, 38*(3), 397–421. https://doi.org/10.1177/0093650210384984
Glasford, D. E., & Calcagno, J. (2012). The conflict of harmony: Intergroup contact, commonality and political solidarity between minority groups. *Journal of Experimental Social Psychology, 48*(1), 323-328. https://doi.org/10.1016/j.jesp.2011.10.001
Global Gender Gap Report. (2021). World Economic Forum. http://www3.weforum.org/docs/WEF_GGGR_2021.pdf
Greenwood, R. M. (2012). Standing at the crossroads: An intersectional approach to women's social identities and political consciousness. In S. Wiley, G. Philogène & T. A. Revenson (Eds.), *Social categories in everyday experience* (pp. 103-129). American Psychological Association. https://doi.org/10.1037/13488-006
Güneş, A., & Ezikoğlu, Ç. (2023). Legal and political challenges of gender equality and crimes against women in Turkey: The question of Istanbul convention. *Women & Criminal Justice, 33*(1), 14-27. https://doi.org/10.1080/08974454.2022.2040695
Kelly, C., & Breinlinger, S. (1995). Identity and injustice: Exploring women's participation in collective action. *Journal of Community & Applied Social Psychology, 5*(1), 41-57. https://doi.org/10.1002/casp.2450050104
Kelly, M. (2015). Feminist identity, collective action, and individual resistance among contemporary U.S. feminists. *Women's Studies International Forum, 48*, 81–92. https://doi.org/10.1016/j.wsif.2014.10.025
Kentmen-Çin, Ç. (2015). Participation in social protests: Comparing Turkey with EU patterns. *Southeast European and Black Sea Studies, 15*(3), 223-237. https://doi.org/10.1080/14683857.2015.1015314
Küçükkırca, İ. A. (2018). The relationality between the 'Free Women's Movement of Kurdistan' and the Feminist Movement in Turkey: Building solidarity or coalition in peace and wartime. In: H. A. Aksöy (ed.), *Patriachat im Wandel: Frauen und Politik in der Türkei* (pp. 133-156). Campus Verlag.
Lee, T. M. L. (2007). Rethinking the personal0 and the political: Feminist activism and civic engagement. *Hypatia, 22*(4), 163-179. https://doi.org/10.1111/j.1527-2001.2007.tb01326.x
Levitsky, S., & Way, L. A. (2002). Elections without democracy: The rise of competitive authoritarianism. *Journal of Democracy, 13*(2), 51-65. https://doi.org/10.1353/jod.2002.0026

McIntosh, P. (1988). White privilege and male privilege: A personal account of coming to see correspondences through work in women's studies (Working Paper No. 189, Center for Research on Women). Wellesley College.

Mikołajczak, G., Becker, J. C., & Iyer, A. (2022). Women who challenge or defend the status quo: Ingroup identities as predictors of progressive and reactionary collective action. *European Journal of Social Psychology, 52*(4), 626-641. https://doi.org/10.1002/ejsp.2842

Mossakowski, K. N., & Zhang, W. (2014). Does social support buffer the stress of discrimination and reduce psychological distress among Asian Americans? *Social Psychology Quarterly, 77*(3), 273–295. https://doi.org/10.1177/0190272514534271

Odağ, Ö., Uluğ, Ö. M., Kanık, B., & Maganić, M. M. (2023). Exploring the Context-Sensitivity of Collective Action Motivations and the Mobilizing Role of Social Media: A Comparative Interview Study With Activists in Germany and Turkey. *Political Psychology, 44*(2), 235-255. https://doi.org/10.1111/pops.12836

Özcan, E. (2018). Conservative women in power: A new predicament for transnational feminist media research. In D. Harp, J. Loke, & I. Bachmann (Eds.), *Feminist approaches to media theory and research* (pp. 167–181). Palgrave Macmillan. https://doi.org/10.1007/978-3-319-90838-0_12

Öztunç, M. (2023). Digital activism in Turkey: Istanbul Convention as a symbol of women's movement. *Turkish Online Journal of Design Art and Communication, 13*(2), 407-423. https://doi.org/10.7456/tojdac.1234097

Painia, B. A. (2018). Feminism and The Black Church: A Qualitative Analysis of Feminism Among Black Women in A Southern Baptist Church [Unpublished doctoral dissertation]. Louisiana State University, USA.

Schuster, J. (2017). Why the personal remained political: comparing second and third wave perspectives on everyday feminism. *Social Movement Studies, 16*(6), 647-659. https://doi.org/10.1080/14742837.2017.1285223

Selvanathan, H. P., Uluğ, Ö. M., & Burrows, B. (2023). What should allies do? Identifying activist perspectives on the role of white allies in the struggle for racial justice in the United States. *European Journal of Social Psychology, 53*(1), 43-60. https://doi.org/10.1002/ejsp.2882

Son, J., & Lin, N. (2008). Social capital and civic action: A network-based approach. *Social Science Research, 37*(1), 330–349. https://doi.org/10.1016/j.ssresearch.2006.12.004

Temoçin, R. (2024). İstanbul Erkek Lisesi öğrencilerinden kadın cinayetleri için sessiz yürüyüş [Silent march by Istanbul Boys High School students for femicides]. *Cumhuriyet*. https://www.cumhuriyet.com.tr/turkiye/istanbul-erkek-lisesi-ogrencilerinden-kadin-cinayetleri-icin-sessiz-2256517

Tropp, L. R., & Uluğ, Ö. M. (2019). Are White women showing up for racial justice? Intergroup contact, closeness to people targeted by prejudice, and collective action. *Psychology of Women Quarterly, 43*(3), 335-347. https://doi.org/10.1177/0361684319840269

Uluğ, Ö. M., & Acar, Y. G. (2014). *Bir olmadan biz olmak: Farklı gruplardan aktivistlerin gözüyle Gezi direnişi* [Becoming us without being one: The Gezi Resistance from the perspective of different activists]. Dipnot Yayınları.

Uluğ, Ö. M., & Acar, Y. G. (2015). 'We are more than alliances between groups': A social psychological perspective on the Gezi Park protesters and negotiating levels of identity. In I. David & K. F. Toktamış (Eds.), *'Everywhere Taksim': Sowing the seeds for a new Turkey at Gezi* (pp. 77–89). Amsterdam University Press. https://doi.org/10.15 15/9789048526390-010

Uluğ, Ö. M., & Acar, Y. G. (2018). What happens after the protests? Understanding protest outcomes through multi-level social change. *Peace and Conflict: Journal of Peace Psychology, 24*(1), 44-53. https://doi.org/10.1037/pac0000269

Uluğ, Ö. M., Acar, Y. G., & Kanık, B. (2021). Reflecting on research: Researcher identity in conflict studies from the perspectives of participants. *European Journal of Social Psychology, 51*(6), 847-861. https://doi.org/10.1002/ejsp.2776

Uluğ, Ö. M., Acar, Y. G., & Kanık, B. (2025). "Is voting even effective?" Examining voting and protest as an expression of dissent and their efficacy in risky contexts. *Analyses of Social Issues and Public Policy.* https://doi.org/10.1111/asap.12445

Uluğ, Ö. M., Chayinska, M., Schreiber, J. A., & Taylor, L. K. (2024). A multi-dimensional typology of allyship action in violent intergroup conflict settings: Differentiating actor, target, and type of action. *European Review of Social Psychology,* 1-46. https://doi.org/10.1080/10463283.2024.2396733

Uluğ, Ö. M., Chayinska, M., & Tropp, L. R. (2022). Conceptual, methodological, and contextual challenges in studying collective action: Recommendations for future research. *TPM: Testing, Psychometrics, Methodology in Applied Psychology, 29*(1), 9–22. https://doi.org/10.4473/TPM29.1.2

Uluğ, Ö. M., Chayinska, M., & Tropp, L. R. (2023). Does witnessing gender discrimination predict women's collective action intentions for gender justice? Examining the moderating role of perceived female support. *Journal of Community & Applied Social Psychology, 33*(2), 501-518. https://doi.org/10.1002/casp.2642

Uluğ, Ö. M., Odağ, Ö., Cohrs, J. C., & Holtz, P. (2017). Understanding the Kurdish conflict through the eyes of Kurds and Turks: New conflict reflections from lay people in Turkey. *nternational Journal of Conflict Management, 28*(4), 483-508. https://doi.org/10.1108/IJCMA-05-2016-0035

Uluğ, Ö. M., Odağ, Ö., & Solak, N. (2020). Women's rights and gender equality in Turkey / Voices against misogyny in Turkey: The case of a successful online collective action against a sexist commercial. *International Journal of Communication, 14,* 5575-5596.

Uluğ, Ö. M., & Tropp, L. R. (2021). Witnessing racial discrimination shapes collective action for racial justice: Enhancing awareness of privilege among advantaged groups. *Journal of Applied Social Psychology, 51*(3), 248-261. https://doi.org/10.1111/jasp.12731

Uysal, M. S., Uluğ, Ö. M., Kanık, B., & Aydemir, A. (2022). "The liberation of LGBTQ+ will also liberate heterosexuals": Heterosexual feminist women's participation in solidarity-based collective action for LGBTQ+ rights. *European Journal of Social Psychology, 52*(2), 377-390. https://doi.org/10.1002/ejsp.2799

Van Zomeren, M., Postmes, T., & Spears, R. (2008). Toward an integrative social identity model of collective action: A quantitative research synthesis of three socio-psychological perspectives. *Psychological Bulletin, 134*(4), 504-535. https://doi.org/10.10 37/0033-2909.134.4.504

Navigating The Developmental Maze: A Feminist Journey through Challenges[1]

Doğa Eroğlu-Şah

European University of Lefke, Northern Cyprus

First and foremost, I must clarify that although the term *developmental* appears in the title, this text does not directly address developmental psychology. Rather, it examines the thesis process I undertook as part of a doctoral program in developmental psychology at a university in Turkey. Morss (1995) underscores the importance of critically examining the implications and meanings associated with the term *development*. According to Morss, adopting a skeptical stance toward development and developmental psychology inevitably raises complex questions. Moreover, those who challenge the foundational assumptions of developmental psychology—assumptions often taken for granted—risk being marginalized within the field and accused of not being 'true' developmental psychologists. My doctoral journey began with precisely the skepticism that Morss describes, leading me into an unforeseen academic labyrinth.

There are many aspects of research that often go unmentioned or cannot be thoroughly discussed in 'scientific' academic studies. The emphasis on presenting research objectively frequently leads to the omission of essential elements crucial for fully understanding the context of our studies. These omissions—including the fundamental assumptions upon which our research is based and the broader contextual factors—are what ultimately impart our work with meaning and significance. In this text, I will reflect on my doctoral thesis process, both in relation to my subjective experiences and my study on masculinities. More specifically, I aim to explore the interactional and intersubjective processes that underpinned my research—processes I was previously required to frame within a positivist paradigm. This narrative will include aspects I consider significant but was unable to incorporate into my thesis report. I will elucidate the evolving interactional process that shaped my research at each stage, using a perspective akin to rotating a kaleidoscope.

---

1   This text is a condensed and revised version of my Turkish chapter, Studying "Masculinity" as a "Woman" and Reflexivity, published in the 2022 book Critical Psychology: Approaches, Agendas, and Debates, edited by U. Şah, A. Gürel-Kayaoğlu, B. Gürsel, D. Eroğlu, and E. Sandıkçı.

By adopting this approach, I will allow myself to be guided by the unfolding encounters and writings that emerge, occasionally acknowledging my own surprise at these revelations. This methodology seeks to convey the fluid and transformative nature of the research experience—an aspect often left undocumented in mainstream academic discourse. If you are ready, I will begin my story!

Most individuals who embark on a scientific study recognize that even at the ideation stage, we are confronted with implicit and explicit requirements. Even before sharing an idea with others, a deeply ingrained framework of expected thought patterns quickly takes hold. If the study is intended for publication in prestigious, academically recognized venues, the challenges become even more pronounced. Often, we must navigate a field shaped by established historical and political frameworks. The extent to which we adhere to these well-trodden paths or seek to forge new ones is a critical consideration. When research is conducted within structured academic programs, such as a master's or doctoral degree—where scholarly inquiry is a requirement—the process inevitably opens the door to countless unforeseen challenges.

You don't necessarily have to pursue radically new paths to encounter these difficulties. Simply pausing for a moment on a well-trodden path that no longer allows for new growth and contemplating the path itself can draw attention. If there is a goal to be achieved, such as graduation or publication, one possible approach is to hold the hand of someone who knows the path, and without letting go, follow the invisible trails beside the path as far as your combined reach allows.

I promised you a journey in the title, didn't I? At this point, I will begin the narration of my journey from its midpoint; after all, the beginning would have led us into entirely different territories. Above all, I must acknowledge that if I managed to make even a little progress on this invisible path I mentioned earlier, it was thanks to my dear thesis advisor and the professors on my supervisory committee. Despite having already expressed my gratitude in the thesis itself and in person, you may wonder why I feel the need to reiterate it in this text. The answer lies in the fact that the middle of my adventure begins with the informal rejection of my thesis proposal on an entirely different subject before it could even be formally presented.

This leads us to the core explanation for why my doctoral thesis focuses on masculinity. Don't get me wrong, it is not that I was reluctant to engage with the subject of masculinity; on the contrary, I was fully aware of the growing yet still limited body of research on masculinity within the field of psychology in Turkey. However, my thesis topic was chosen due to concerns about how it might reconcile with an approach that is not particularly open to moving beyond the positivist paradigm. You likely thought that the phrase 'not particularly open' was an understatement even before I mentioned it. Additionally, you might have observed my shift from the first-person narrative to the passive construction in 'was chosen.' My aim here is not to initiate a debate about paradigms but to underscore the point that, as doctoral candidates, we often find ourselves unable to choose even a paradigm, let alone a research topic, as the foundation of our work. The hierarchical and ideological academic structures and relationships that dictate the basis of what appears to be our own research are what I wish to draw attention to. Consequently, my thesis advisor and I navigated the entire thesis process under the shadow of those who imposed the positivist paradigm upon us, leveraging their authority. We found solace in the prospect that upon completing the doctorate, in other words, after liberating myself from the university—the very institution that represents 'academic freedom'—I would finally have the opportunity to pursue research topics and methodologies of my own choosing.

Throughout the thesis, I attempted to subtly integrate the social constructionist perspective, to which I feel more closely aligned. This was far from easy. However, the challenge was not only to conceal my approach from the institution or department that imposes the mainstream discourse. I think the hardest part was hiding from myself. I often found myself writing explanations that I did not fully agree with or glossing over points without offering criticism, all while trying to ignore my own way of making sense of the world. Consequently, I found myself either unable to express what I genuinely wanted to write or feeling compelled to withhold my actual perspective. I set aside many critical feminist studies that I encountered during my literature review, intending to read them after completing my thesis. Reading these works made it nearly impossible for me to continue with my thesis. At this point, my thesis advisor and the professors on my supervisory committee provided me with every possible opportunity to express myself, offering both academic and personal support. Nevertheless, my professors, along with me, faced various challenges at different levels and in different forms.

I anticipate that you may have stories similar to those I have recounted so far, or perhaps even ones that make you think, "this is nothing compared to what I've experienced." I have personally heard some of these stories from researchers who have faced or are currently facing various challenges during their research process, while others I learned about through secondhand stories. At times, I found myself feeling 'grateful' that my experiences were not as severe as those of others, because there were indeed 'worse' situations. However, these narratives often portrayed 'unfortunate' events befalling 'individuals.' Consequently, the direct and covert interventions of hierarchical institutional structures and intra-departmental relationships aimed at aligning students and academics can be viewed as 'normal' components of educational programs. Moreover, such experiences in the research process can be effortlessly detached from the research itself (topic, method, report, etc.), as if they were unrelated. My aim in writing this is to take a step away from the notion that "this is just what it means to pursue a master's or PhD," to resist the normalization of institutional impositions through the discourse of 'common experiences' or the personalization of these impositions as 'isolated incidents,' and to contribute further to the politicization of this process.

Now, I shift my kaleidoscope to a different perspective on this process— one grounded in institutional power dynamics. This perspective pertains to some of my experiences that took place shortly after my research topic was chosen.

Flux and Reflux: Between Positivism and Social Constructionism

While I was preoccupied with the dynamics of institutional power relations (given that the allotted time for writing a thesis proposal was six months, and I ended up having to write two), we had already chosen a research topic. I found myself staring at my thesis title—*Analysis of the Relationship of Gender Stress, System Justification, and Sexism in Men* (Eroğlu-Şah, 2020)— as if I hadn't written the proposal myself. Although we only included participants who identified their sexual orientation as heterosexual and their gender as men, we intentionally omitted 'heterosexual' from the title because we had heard that another thesis proposal with 'heterosexual' in its title had failed to gain approval from the university's ethics committee. I consoled myself with the thought that at least I wasn't compelled to use the original theoretical term *Male Gender Role Stress* (Eisler & Blalock, 1991; Eisler & Skidmore, 1987). My concern here was with the concept of 'role'. I was aware that the concept of role had been critiqued by some feminist theorists (Stone, 2007) and that it was considered insufficient, reductive, and simplistic for addressing gender (Connell, 2005).

Another concern of mine was that my research topic ultimately revolved around the 'challenges' heterosexual men experience in relation to their gender. A historical framework that fueled this concern was already present. Bozok (2013) discusses how studies on masculinities[2] have been approached

---

2   Masculinities: The adoption of this concept is considered a significant turning point, particularly in the transition from a singular masculinity to multiple masculinities (Smiler, 2004). Raewyn Connell pioneered this shift with the concepts of masculinities and hegemonic masculinity. This approach posits that, rather than a universal, uniform masculinity, there are diverse constructions of masculinity, necessitating the discussion of multiple masculinities. Masculinities are further diversified through intersections with gender, class, and race. Thus, the concept of masculinities indicates a changeable construct rather than a fixed one, varying according to historical, cultural, social, contextual, and geographical conditions

through masculinist, men's liberationist, queer, and (pro)feminist perspectives. Bozok proposes this classification based on the relationship between masculinity studies, patriarchy, and feminism. Let me briefly explain these approaches.

Firstly, masculinist approaches aim to directly perpetuate patriarchal ideology and the heteronormative structure. This perspective positions itself against feminism and queer theory, which are perceived as threats to the dominant status of (heterosexual) men within the social structure, and it normalizes heterosexual masculinity as the norm. This process of normalization may be accompanied by explanations rooted in biological determinism and/or religious discourse. Additionally, it justifies sexism by placing heterosexual masculinity in a superior position within a hierarchical gender system, thereby regarding others as inferior.

Men's liberationist approaches, on the other hand, argue that patriarchy oppresses not only women but also men and aim to liberate men from the harms of patriarchy. In other words, they seek to emancipate men from patriarchal constraints. While these approaches differ from masculinist perspectives in terms of their relationship with patriarchy, they have primarily focused on the oppression of men by patriarchy and have notably distanced themselves from feminism. Finally, queer and (pro)feminist approaches, which pursue a different path from both masculinist and men's liberationist approaches in terms of their relationship with patriarchy, aim for a reflexive critique of masculinities, positioning themselves against patriarchal ideology under the guidance of feminism and queer studies. In other words, in their struggle against patriarchy, they also focus on men's role in producing this system (Bozok, 2009, 2011, 2013).

From the perspective outlined by Bozok, we can note that the second wave feminist movement of the 1960s and 1970s profoundly influenced how masculinity was addressed within the field of Psychology[3], leading the discipline to shift its focus toward men in response to the feminist critique of that era (Edley, 2017). However, this approach to understanding masculinity originates precisely from the men's liberationist perspectives that Bozok describes. In other words, the central argument of these early masculinity studies was that gender norms negatively affect men just as much as they do women (Bozok,

---

(Connell, 2005). This approach is made possible by feminist theories that posit multiple constructions of femininity rather than a singular one (Stone, 2007). It is important to note that Hearn suggests the concept(s) used to unify studies on masculinities should reflect that the field of masculinity studies is not separate from feminist studies (Akşit & Varışlı, 2014).
3   Psychology is capitalized to indicate the institutional structure of the discipline.

2009, 2011, 2013; Sancar, 2016). Indeed, this area of study was even referred to as 'the psychology of men'[4] at that time.

Although my approach does not align with men's liberationist perspectives, I was concerned that examining the difficulties heterosexual men face due to their gender might be misunderstood as implying an equivalence between men's and women's experiences or might inadvertently steer the research in that direction. At the outset of this study, I was uncertain about how freely I could articulate my own perspective on the issue. The prospect of relying on a theoretical framework I had critically examined was particularly challenging, as it risked perpetuating the very power structures my research sought to interrogate.

Many critical researchers advocate for an approach that recognizes the active role of the individual in the construction of gender (Bora & Üstün, 2005; Burr, 2003; Clarke & Braun, 2009; Edley, 2001; Seymour-Smith, 2017). This brings us to a key point McCarry (2007) highlights regarding masculinities: men should not be regarded as victims of masculinity; rather, studies should aim to make both masculinity as a phenomenon and men's practices visible.

From my perspective, it was crucial to study the discourse and practices of men, as primary agents in the construction of masculinity, without obscuring their role in this process. Thus, the stress heterosexual men experience regarding their gender emerges not merely as 'experiences of difficulty' that befall them but as something that actively involves their agency in producing and maintaining patriarchal ideology. Simultaneously, the ideological dimension of these seemingly individual and psychological difficulties becomes evident.

Consider the possibilities of conducting a psychology doctoral study that directly or indirectly problematizes these issues in an environment where individualism and psychologization—both foundational to the psychology discipline—are staunchly defended. When the defense of the positivist paradigm becomes personalized, institutional power dynamics may function in a way

---

4   Ronald Levant proposed the establishment of a separate division within the American Psychological Association (APA) dedicated to studying the 'the psychology of men.' In response, he was met with the ironic question, "Isn't the entire field of psychology already about men's psychology?" (Levant & Wong, 2017, p. 3). This question underscores the notion that, as in many other fields, men have historically been considered the normative standard in psychology, a perspective that continues to persist in various ways and at different levels. Since the establishment of this separate division (Division 51) in 1995, the work within the APA has adopted a critical perspective, influenced by feminism, queer theory, and masculinity studies. Particularly, the contributions of research informed by intersectionality, multiculturalism, and social constructionist approaches have played a crucial role in the transformations within this field. Nevertheless, this area is still referred to as the 'psychology of men and masculinities' (Levant & Wong, 2017).

that, regardless of whom you cite to support your arguments, anything you say can be turned into evidence against you in favor of the positivist paradigm!

In addition to all of this, the fact that the doctoral thesis process—which I began with the excitement of conducting discourse analysis—ultimately left me dealing with scales, was an entirely different issue. As we had started working with a quantitative research model, I was uncomfortable examining this issue through the lens of attitudes.

I was aware that attempting to understand phenomena solely at the level of attitudes and behaviors was insufficient for meaningful explanation (Aygül, 2016; Potter & Wetherell, 1987). After all, examining a phenomenon through attitudes inherently lacks context. Moreover, the scales used in research to measure attitudes inevitably shape the phenomenon in line with the scale's development objectives, thereby restricting its meaning to a predefined framework. The construction of this framework became a critical issue. However, this does not prevent scales from being presented as 'neutral' measurement tools. At this point, Smiler (2004) highlights that measurement tools should not only serve as instruments in research but should also be subjects of investigation themselves—a perspective that offers solace to researchers who approach scales with skepticism.

Fortunately, the acceptance of mixed-methods studies within the mainstream paradigm had increased. Thus, anticipating that a mixed-methods approach would be institutionally recognized, we incorporated qualitative data into the research. Initially, we structured the mixed-method design so that qualitative data would support quantitative data. This is likely not surprising. This was because quantitative research, in which scales were the data collection tool, was still at the forefront, and no one could object.

However, 'fortunately,' the results of the quantitative research seemed likely to be weak or insufficient. The quantitative part of the study could, at most, demonstrate a specific relationship between gender-based stress, justification of the gender system, and sexism in heterosexual men in emerging adulthood[5], but it couldn't explain how men experience and make sense of these phenomena. If heterosexual men in emerging adulthood were encountering difficulties related to their gender, what were these areas of difficulty? How did they justify the current binary gender system? How did they position themselves within this system? Quantitative research was unable to address these questions, yet qualitative research, particularly through in-depth, face-to-face interviews, could provide insights into these and similar questions, albeit to a

---

5   At this point, it would be appropriate to provide an overview of the participants in my study. The participants were fourth-year undergraduate students, aged 18 to 30, who self-identified as men in gender and heterosexual in sexual orientation. They were predominantly middle-class, white, and enrolled in social sciences. The participants represented a range of religious beliefs, ethnic backgrounds, political views, and socioeconomic statuses.

limited extent. Consequently, in our revised research model, qualitative research was elevated to an 'equivalent' status with quantitative research (in fact, it later overshadowed the quantitative research—but let's keep that between us).

Amid the meaninglessness and pessimism of questioning, "Why am I doing this study?" while conducting a quantitative study that was not my own preference, the prospect of conducting a standalone qualitative study was like a gray light after a downpour. However, through experience, I later came to understand the inherent challenges and, ultimately, the impossibility of reconciling positivist and social constructionist paradigms (Stainton-Rogers, 2003).

From Instrument to Purpose: The Transformative Possibilities of the Interview

I was incredibly excited after conducting my first face-to-face interview. In fact, these interviews allowed me to establish a meaningful connection with my research. I began to recognize that the interview held potential beyond merely serving as a data collection instrument. After a few interviews, I recorded the following reflection:

> "This is my first research experience involving face-to-face interviews. While I had a theoretical understanding, firsthand engagement in this process was entirely different. For those familiar with qualitative research, this may not be new, but I found that the interviews themselves had a transformative effect during the conversations. They functioned not merely as a source of data but as an act of transformation—more as a purpose than a tool. Regardless of the research outcome, I felt as though I had contributed, even in a small way, to feminism through these interviews, and this brought me joy. For me, the significance of this study lies not only in its academic contribution but also in its relevance to the feminist movement."

During the interviews, some participants questioned their actions and perspectives as men. Some participants stated that their initial motivation for joining the interview was self-confrontation or a personal challenge, and they described the experience as a 'gain' for themselves. One participant even noted that while he found anonymity comforting, he would have no objection to me revealing his identity if I wished; he was willing to face any consequences that might follow. For some, merely participating in such a study was seen as a sign that they were approaching masculinity from a critical perspective. Another participant took pride in sharing things that other men 'wouldn't dare' to talk about. For others, the 'academically purposed interview' became a space for confession and self-disclosure about their masculinity, as everything they shared would contribute to the research. While responding to my questions, some participants carefully managed the masculinity they projected, often emphasizing that they 'of course support women's rights and oppose violence against women'. However, after a while, some of these participants began to struggle to keep track of their own narratives.

I suspect this breaking point may be particularly revealing for many researchers. In my study, this breaking point was valuable because aspects of masculinity that participants sought to conceal emerged involuntarily in the flow of conversation. It was particularly meaningful for me to observe that, even when participants thought they were distancing themselves from patriarchal discourse, they were, in fact, still speaking from within that very discourse. At this point, it is also worth noting that some men who have written texts critiquing their own masculinity—assuming they later reread their work—similarly take pride in the (pro-)feminist stance they believe they have adopted, assuming they have stepped beyond patriarchal discourse.

However, I did not fully leverage the transformative potential of the interviews. Our aim in this study was to explore the participants' experiences and their own meaning-making, which led us to follow a different path from research methods that explicitly pursue a transformative goal during the interviews themselves, such as participatory action research (Öztan, 2015). Conversely, in the face-to-face interviews I conducted for my thesis, participants spoke extensively while I asked questions with minimal verbal commentary. The researcher's choice to refrain from expressing their own views during an interview certainly has implications for the research. Typically, the methodological aim is to minimize these effects to avoid influencing the participant, thereby allowing the researcher to capture the participant's own interpretations and meaning-making of the topics discussed (Yıldırım & Şimşek, 2013). By doing so, we may assume the role of a 'listener' who is almost exempt from active participation in the conversation; thus, we find ourselves in the 'safe zone of objectivity' within qualitative research methods, albeit not to the same extent as in quantitative research! If, like me, you hear a participant say, "You did a great job of staying neutral," then you know you have succeeded!

Asserting that the researcher makes the study more objective by remaining in the background during the interview is not particularly aligned with a social constructionist approach. The way an interview is structured indeed influences the interaction between the interviewer and the participant. Hmm, perhaps even referring to the interview as an 'interaction' is insufficient; it seems like we still haven't fully distanced ourselves from the positivist paradigm yet, don't you think? In that case, let's set aside the notions of 'influence' and 'interaction' and put it this way: Inevitably, the various discursive resources we draw upon—whether or not I explicitly voice my opinions—serve as a foundation for the interview in multiple ways. My choice of topic, facial expressions, listening style, the way I respond as a listener, my tone of voice, and the fact that participants perceive or categorize me as a (feminist) woman, whether I state it or not—all these elements were the basis of how the interview itself unfolded. These were not external variables affecting the interview; rather, they constituted the ever-evolving foundation upon which we constructed meaning throughout the conversation.

Considering masculinity as a performance during conversation is crucial as it enables us to discuss different interactions and the various representations that emerge throughout these interactions (Seymour-Smith, 2017). In this way, the masculinity we focus on during the interview, as a gender category, appears not as a natural and fixed reality but as a performative construction. This construction refers to a process collectively undertaken with others (Burr, 2003; Edley, 2001; West & Zimmerman, 1987), including me during the interview. In other words, the participants did not simply convey their individual worlds of meaning to me in isolation; rather, within the interaction and by drawing from different discursive resources, they were reconstructing and reinterpreting their masculinities with me during the interviews. In a sense, they re-narrated their previous experiences.

Interestingly, most participants agreed that these interactional interviews felt like casual conversations. Indeed, this is one of the primary objectives of conducting in-depth interviews; a skilled interviewer moves away from a question-answer format, creating a conversational atmosphere where the participant often forgets they are in a research setting and that their words are being recorded for the interview. In the interviews, some participants reported almost forgetting they were in an interview for academic research. However, the most striking among these was a participant's statement that "we mutually shared our thoughts." Now, we could attribute the participant's approach to what we just discussed—the inevitably interactional nature of the process, which stemmed from my presence as a researcher and my skills as an effective interviewer. But I suggest we refrain from doing so. The fact that I conducted interviews with heterosexual men, that the focus was on masculinity, and that most participants pointed out my being a woman, provides important context for understanding what it means that I didn't express my opinions during the interviews and why they felt conversational. Let's not overlook this. To illustrate, let me refer to what the participants said:

> "There are no judgmental questions, just more thought-provoking ones... I mean, listening sincerely and nicely with respect and a smile, this is really, you know, a good thing, I am comfortable and free, there's absolutely no limitation in the questions, no interruption, I mean it's nice, I enjoyed the interview; if interviews were like this, I mean, it could go on until morning, I'd talk and listen."

> "I think it's more related to the other person staying neutral—the interviewer staying neutral. You remained as neutral as possible in this matter, and it made me comfortable. That's why, you know, I may have said some critical things about

women, maybe things you wouldn't like, but because these continued naturally within the conversation, it wasn't a problem—I spoke openly."

I think there is no harm in slightly lifting the veil on these participant statements. The interview, in which a woman (that would be me) listened to them with a 'smile,' 'without judgment,' and 'almost as if in agreement,' resembled the 'conversations' they often turned into monologues in their everyday interactions with women. I refrained from counter-arguing, allowing them to speak freely about their discriminatory discourses and practices. At this point, the interaction differed from the debates they typically had with feminists, who in everyday conversations did not usually remain silent in response to their comments. One participant, who had previously debated feminist friends, confided in me about matters he could not express in their presence and freely criticized them in an interview where they could not respond. This extended session of unburdening and confession concluded with the participant declaring, "Hands up! I surrender!" At that moment, I realized that I was perceived as the 'good-natured' feminist in their eyes.

It is well-established that feminism does not exist in a single form; rather, it encompasses a variety of feminist approaches that have branched out and evolved over time. Some of these approaches have been retrospectively labeled, while others are umbrella terms employed by feminists themselves to articulate their positions. However, in contrast to academic and historical terminology, everyday usage tends to be more simplistic. I am certain that you have encountered (or perhaps even used) the expressions 'good feminist' and 'bad feminist.' Typically, those who pose even the slightest threat to the status quo of patriarchy—or might be perceived as doing so—are quickly labeled as 'bad' or even 'man-hating' feminists. In contrast, those who quietly advocate for equal rights without pushing for more, often seen as harmless and unassuming, are labeled as 'good' feminists. Edley and Wetherell's (2001) study, which examines how men discursively construct feminism and feminists, effectively elucidates this phenomenon. The researchers identified the explanations they encountered in men's discourses regarding feminism and feminists as a "Jekyll and Hyde"[6] dichotomy. Within these interpretative repertoires, on one side are the "benign" and "reasonable" feminists who solely seek gender equality, while on the other side are the "monstrous," "irrational," and "crazy" feminists. Indeed, in my own interviews, I encountered similar discourses from participants regarding feminists.

***

---

6   Edley and Wetherell (2001) refer to the Scottish author Robert Louis Stevenson's 1886 novel, Strange Case of Dr. Jekyll and Mr. Hyde.

I must acknowledge the challenging nature of being exposed to participants' discriminatory discourses—rooted in patriarchal ideology—throughout the interviews, as well as silently listening to certain practices involving discrimination, sexism, and/or violence. This feeling persisted through the verbatim transcription process after the interviews and the repeated readings to identify codes and themes within the transcripts. The difficulty stemmed from the silence. For me, analyzing these transcripts was, within the scope of my research, an opportunity to engage in a dialogue with the data—in a sense, with the participants—and ultimately to find my own voice. This, in turn, revealed the transformative impact of this research on me. Recognizing that my voice emerged more strongly as I wrote the discussion section of my research may well mark the beginning of my feminist journey. In her book *Living a Feminist Life*, Sara Ahmed emphasizes the importance of where and through whom we discover feminism: "Feminism as a collective movement is made out of how we are moved to become feminists in dialogue with others" (Ahmed, 2017, p. 5). Just as I write this retrospective sentence about my feminist journey, I am embracing my own feminist stance and voice for the first time—made possible by the voice and efforts of feminist movements that have permeated into me until now. You may perceive this disclosure as 'emotional' and as deviating from 'academic' discourse. However, in solidarity with Sara Ahmed's "killjoy" approach and drawing strength from her, I deliberately position these emotions at the center of this text about my research, sensing that it is only now that the text makes sense. At the same time, I remember reflexivity is a never-ending process.

Position Spectrum

"How do I position myself? How do participants position me? How do I think participants position me? How do I position the participants? How do participants position themselves? How do I think participants position themselves?" You may have noticed how far this line of questioning can extend. But fear not, I'll stop here, as it makes my head spin as well. However, this never-ending stream of questions has instilled in me a sense of ethical responsibility. At this point, I can say that the ongoing flow of questions and my efforts to maintain reflexivity has kept me within a general framework. Reflexivity is, after all, a continuous state of flux; it cannot be captured once and for all. For this reason, I chose to conceptualize this as a position spectrum. Throughout a study, our position remains fluid; in other words, we do not hold a fixed position. At this point, I believe that reflexivity fundamentally represents a persistent ethical endeavor. As Braun and Clarke (2006) state, what is crucial here is the researcher's ability to provide an explanation for what they do and why, and to own these as decisions.

This has been an incredibly challenging process because setting aside the claim of objectivity means confronting ourselves. This requires taking responsibility for our decisions. I realized that my interpretation of participants' statements shifted across the interview, transcription, and analysis stages. For example, while the interaction—the state of being together—was central during the interviews, what lingered during the analysis were the traces of those interactions. As a result, even though the statements in the interviews and the transcripts appeared identical, the fact that they involved different experiences led me to interpret them differently. Recognizing the impact of repeatedly reading the transcripts alone, along with the lingering traces of the interviews that stayed with me, was crucial to the analysis.

During analysis, I found myself increasingly confronted with a distinct feeling. Ultimately, analysis is an interpretative process that systematically deconstructs and integrates data. In this context, participants' explanations and discourse undergo a filtering process. While the data at hand progresses toward meaningful wholes and deepens through our interpretative lens, the filtered-out remnants of conversations that fail to fit within that wholeness increasingly feel like a loss. I came to describe this feeling and experience during the process as *analysis melancholy*.

Conversely, although I engaged in dialogue with the transcripts during analysis, the participants themselves no longer had the opportunity to speak or respond. This rigorous process of repeatedly reading and analyzing the transcripts raised concerns about potentially doing injustice to the participants. It is understandable to feel such concerns during any analysis, as they are closely related to the responsibility we feel to conduct a thorough and in-depth examination of the data. However, this concern must be contextualized within the framework of the research itself.

My primary concern, particularly in relation to 'men,' was the frequent accusation that feminists are merely 'looking for flaws' in everything they do. Throughout the analysis, I constantly asked myself, "Am I looking for flaws in the participants' statements?" I persistently asked myself this question out of fear that my analysis might be dismissed as 'flaw-finding,' which could discredit the discourses and practices I sought to illuminate. At the time, I valued this 'well-intentioned' approach, linking it to my desire to contribute—even in a small way—to the feminist movement. However, I now realize that in asking this question, I was not challenging this ideological accusation against feminists; rather, I accepted, legitimized, and reinforced it. My only consolation in having asked, "Am I looking for flaws?" is that each time I asked it, I was still able to answer, "no."

***

The question "Why did you choose this topic?" often reflects an interest in understanding the researcher's relationship with the subject matter or how the researcher positions themselves in relation to it. However, at times, this question signifies more than a simple curiosity and can carry various meanings depending on the research topic. In the context of my research, the factor that intervened between 'why' and 'topic' was my gender. Thus, the question transformed into "Why —as a woman— did you choose this topic?"

We live in a gendered world, which is commonly constructed through the gender binary instead of a continuum (Clarke & Braun, 2009; Edley, 2017). Therefore, the gender of a researcher studying masculinities becomes a point of interest for 'many'. As a 'woman,' my gendered positioning—and the ways in which it was constructed in relation to participants—were central to my research focus. Additionally, along with my thesis committee, I evaluated the potential advantages and disadvantages of conducting face-to-face interviews with heterosexual men as a woman. This consideration stems from the understanding that our genders are not fixed, natural realities but rather constructions performed discursively (Burr, 2003; Edley, 2001; West & Zimmerman, 1987). Consequently, the face-to-face interviews I conducted became a process where both the participants and I collectively reproduced these constructions. At this point, it was critical to consider that gender cannot be constructed in isolation (Clarke & Braun, 2009). To move beyond merely assuming what my being a woman might signify to the participants, I asked them directly at the end of the interviews.

So far, everything seems to be on track, and my goal remains to make my research as nuanced and insightful as possible. So, let's talk more explicitly about the individuals who prompted the single quotation of the word 'many' above. You know, those who are passionate about their research often do something specific: they discuss their work with colleagues and engage in conversations about it. Discussing our work can be incredibly helpful for gaining direction and clarifying our thoughts. Moreover, exchanging ideas is valuable because it introduces different perspectives. During one of these conversations with a colleague, I encountered this reaction:

> You? Studying the challenges men face? You? How are you going to study men? Hold on, now I'm curious—tell me exactly what your topic is. What are you going to work on? (...) Now, dear Doğa, let's set political correctness aside for a moment—you are a WOMAN. How are you going to understand what we go through? You can't know. You don't have the experience. How do you plan to work on experiences you haven't lived?

Before analyzing these statements, I need to provide some context regarding my colleague. This colleague, a psychologist, is well aware of debates around gender and the idea that it is a relational construct. Nor are they unaware that, in any research, positionality is critically important. As a psychologist, they counsel individuals whose experiences differ from their own and have often expressed opinions on topics they haven't personally experienced. If someone were to say to them, "We can never speak about things we haven't experienced," they would surely recognize the absurdity of that statement. However, when it came to 'masculinity,' their remarks were deeply embedded in patriarchal assumptions. I am certain you also noticed the patronizing tone when they tried to 'put me in my place' as a woman. At this point, I cannot help but provide an example from one of my interviews. In one of the conversations, a participant said the following: "(...) because you, too, are an insightful woman, it must be gratifying for you to hear the masculine perspective from a man."

Let's return to my colleague. They could have conveyed these points to you directly during a scientific meeting. This is the same colleague who, in that setting, could emphasize the importance of challenging the gender binary and assert the necessity of a feminist analysis of masculinities. Yet, outside an academic setting, they did not hesitate to dismiss all of this as 'political correctness.' Part of this accusation of political correctness pointed to the 'fact' that, even though I did not declare myself a woman, it was 'as plain as day' that I was one. Therefore, the implication was that I should not complicate the matter by bringing up the intricate nature of gender identity with a counter-argument like, "Wait a minute, you're assuming I'm a woman—how do you know that?" Such an argument would have necessitated discussing the very foundations of gender ideology. In their view, we should abandon political correctness and address the issue 'plainly'—through a fixed, binary gender ideology—by questioning how I, as a 'woman,' could possibly study 'masculinity,' which 'naturally' excludes me!

In Lieu of a Conclusion

Often, the closing of a text is marked by the phrase 'in conclusion.' However, stating that I've reached the end of this text in such a manner would not suit its language, content, or purpose. From a theoretical standpoint, there is nothing that requires summarization or closure. Instead, I can articulate the final phase of the *beginning* to which my PhD journey has led me.

In the end, despite harboring internal paradigm contradictions, what emerged was a study on masculinity that sought to align as closely as possible with the social constructionist paradigm. Considering the thesis proposal process, which previously forced me into serious self-censorship and even prevented me from using the word 'feminist,' I can say that I was relatively 'free' in the research report.

The 'reflexivity' section was one of the most exciting and intriguing aspects of my thesis. I am thrilled to expand what was previously just a few pages into a full-fledged discussion in this book. As previously mentioned, I documented the dynamic, interactive process that evolved throughout each stage of the research. Like a kaleidoscope, I shifted perspectives within a structured framework, allowing emergent ideas to unfold in writing—often to my own surprise. If asked to rewrite, the kaleidoscope would turn differently, potentially leading to entirely new discussions. For now, I will lean back and look at this temporary appearance as it emerges.

References

Ahmed, S. (2017). *Living a feminist life*. Duke University Press.
Akşit, G., & Varışlı, B. (2014). Studying critical men and masculinities within feminism in Turkey: An interview with Jeff Hearn on transnational approaches to men and masculinities. *Fe Dergi*, 6(2), 81-86.
Aygül, Z. (2016). Psikoloji araştırmalarında cinsiyetçilik: Cinsiyetçiliği incelemenin cinsiyetçiliği [Sexism in psychology research: The sexism of studying sexism] In S. A. Arkonaç (Ed.), *Söylem Araştırmaları [Discourse Studies]* (pp. 211-234). Hiperlink, İstanbul.
Bora, A., & Üstün, İ. (2005). *Sıcak aile ortamı: demokratikleşme sürecinde kadın ve erkekler [Warm family atmosphere: Women and men in the democratization process]*. TESEV. https://www.tesev.org.tr/tr/research/sicak-aile-ortami-demokratikles me-surecinde-kadin-ve-erkekler/
Bozok, M. (2009). Feminizmin erkekler cephesindeki yankısı: Erkekler ve erkeklik üzerine eleştirel incelemeler. [The echo of feminism on the men's front: Critical examinations on men and masculinities]. *Cogito, 58,* 269-284.
Bozok, M. (2011). *Masculinities with questions and answers.* SOGEP.
Bozok, M. (2013). *Constructing local masculinities: A case study from Trabzon, Turkey.* (Publication No. 345589) [Doctoral dissertation, Middle East Technical University]. YÖK Tez Merkezi https://tez.yok.gov.tr/UlusalTezMerkezi/
Braun, V., & Clarke, V. (2006). Using thematic analysis in psychology, *Qualitative Research in Psychology, 3*(2), 77-101.
Burr, V. (2003). *Social constructionism* (2nd ed.). Routledge.
Clarke, V., & Braun, V. (2009). Gender. In D. Fox, I. Prilleltensky, & S. Austin (Eds.), *Critical Psychology: An Introduction* (2nd ed., pp. 232-249). Sage. https://books.google. com.tr/books?id=zbTYJ2Mz9jQC&printsec=frontcover&hl=tr#v=onepage&q&f= false
Connell, R. W. (2005). *Masculinities*. University of California Press.
Edley, N. (2001). Analysing masculinity: Interpretative repertoires, ideological dilemmas and subject positions. In M. Wetherell, S. Taylor, & S. J. Yates (Ed.), *Discourse as data: A guide to analysis* (pp.189–228). Sage and the Open University.
Edley, N. (2017). *Men and masculinity: The basics*. Routledge.
Edley, N. & Wetherell, M. (2001). Jekyll and Hyde: Men's constructions of feminism and feminists. *Feminism & Psychology, 11*(4), 439–457.
Eisler, R. M. & Blalock, J. A. (1991). Masculine gender role stress: Implications for the assessment of men. *Clinical Psychology Review, 11*(1), 45–60.

Eisler, R. M. & Skidmore, J. R. (1987). Masculine gender role stress: Scale development and component factors in the appraisal of stressful situations. *Behavior Modification*, *11*(2), 123-136.

Eroğlu-Şah, D. (2020). *Analysis of the Relationship of Gender Stress, System Justification and Sexism in Men*, (Publication No. 660331) [Doctoral dissertation, Maltepe Üniversitesi, İstanbul]. YÖK Tez Merkezi. https://tez.yok.gov.tr/UlusalTezMerkezi/

Levant, R. F. & Wong, Y. J. (2017). Introduction: Maturation of the psychology of men and masculinities. In R. F. Levant & Y. J. Wong (Eds.), *The psychology of men and masculinities* (pp. 3–11). American Psychological Association.

McCarry, M. (2007). Masculinity studies and male violence: Critique or collusion? *Women's Studies International Forum*, *30*(5), 404–415.

Morss J. R. (1995). *Growing Critical: Alternatives to developmental psychology.* London: Routledge.

Öztan, E. (2015). Feminist araştırmalar ve yöntem [Feminist research and methodology]. In F. Saygılıgil (Ed.), *Toplumsal cinsiyet tartışmaları [Gender debates]* (pp. 271-289).

Potter, J. & Wetherell, M. (1987). *Discourse and social psychology: Beyond attitudes and behaviour.* Sage.

Sancar, S. (2016). *Erkeklik: İmkansız iktidar:Ailede, piyasada ve sokakta erkekler [Masculinity: Impossible power: Men in the family, the market, and the street]* (4th ed.). İstanbul: Metis Yayıncılık.

Seymour-Smith, S. (2017). A critical discursive approach to studying masculinities. In R. F. Levant & Y. J. Wong (Ed.), *The psychology of men and masculinities* (pp. 105–138). American Psychological Association.

Stainton-Rogers, W. (2003). *Social Psychology: Experimental and Critical Approaches.* Open University Press.

Smiler, A. P. (2004). Thirty years after the discovery of gender: Psychological concepts and measures of masculinity. *Sex Roles: A Journal of Research*, *50*(1-2), 15–26.

Stone, A. (2007). *An Introduction to Feminist Philosophy.* Malden, MA: Polity.

West, C. & Zimmerman, D., H. (1987). Doing gender. *Gender & Society*, *1*(2), 125–151.

Yıldırım, A., & Şimşek, H. (2013). *Sosyal bilimlerde nitel araştırma yöntemleri [Qualitative research methods in social sciences].* Ankara: Seçkin Yayıncılık.

Authors

Dr. Büşra Yalçınöz Uçan

Büşra Yalcınöz-Uçan is a clinical psychologist and works as a research associate at Saint Mary's University, NS, Canada, as part of the Gender-based Violence-Migration (GBV-MIG) Canada Research Program. She was the Marie Curie postdoctoral fellow at the Department of Media and Social Sciences, University of Stavanger, Norway. Her research project investigated the transformative use of digital technologies in the context of gender-based violence and immigration. Yalcınöz-Uçan was a postdoctoral researcher at the Department of Psychology at the University of Waterloo, Canada. As a part of this research fellowship, she worked on a community partnership project examining the availability, accessibility, and effectiveness of trauma-informed psychological interventions and support programs in the gender-based violence sector in Canada. Yalcınöz-Uçan completed her Ph.D. in 2019 at the Department of Clinical Psychology, Boğaziçi University, Turkey. Her Ph.D. research focused on women's decision-making and safety-seeking strategies in violent relationships and utilized a feminist intersectionality approach.

Leyla Soydinç

Leyla Soydinç graduated from Yeditepe University's Psychology Department in 2012. Between 2013 and 2015, she worked as a psychologist in the social support units and shelter of a municipality. From 2015 to 2018, she led the Gender Mainstreaming Program within a youth NGO. She conducted educational studies and advocacy on gender, gender-based violence, dating violence, and methods of struggling mechanisms. She obtained her master's degrees in Psychological Trauma from Kocaeli University and Women's Studies from Istanbul University with the theses "The Effect of Women's Shelters on Women's Mental Health" and "Feminist Model Discussions for Women's Shelters in Turkey," respectively. After becoming a volunteer at Mor Çatı-Purple Roof Women's Shelter Foundation during her student years, she worked in the shelter from 2018 to 2020. Since 2020, she has continued her work with women within the scope of psychological support work at Mor Çatı and has been giving part-time lectures at Yeditepe University. Her clinical and academic studies focus on violence against women, psychological first aid, self-care and boundaries for trauma workers, feminist social and psychological support work, women's shelters, feminist psychotherapy, and related feminist policies.

Prof. Dr. Şahika Yüksel

Şahika Yüksel graduated from the Istanbul University Medical Faculty and worked for many decades in the Department of Psychiatry there. Her clinical specialization, research, and professional focus include addressing post-traumatic issues, particularly among women subjected to psychological, physical, and sexual violence in domestic settings and detention. She has also collaborated with non-governmental organizations on rehabilitation centers for torture survivors and shelters for women who have experienced sexual and physical violence. Additionally, her work spans areas such as mass violence resulting from bombings, suicide attacks, and large-scale accidents, as well as providing counseling and affirmative therapy for LGBT and transgender individuals and their families.

Yüksel is the founder and consultant of the Mor Çatı - Purple Roof Women's Shelter Foundation, as well as the founder of the Turkish Human Rights Foundation and the European Society for Traumatic Stress Studies. She was honored with the 2020 WPATH Harry Benjamin Lifetime Distinguished Advocacy Award and received the 2019 Distinguished Publication Award from the Association for Women in Psychology for her article titled "Genocidal Sexual Assault on Women and the Role of Culture in the Rehabilitation Process: Experiences from Working with Yazidi Women in Turkey," published in the journal *Torture* in 2018.

Dr. Ayşe Dayı

Ayşe Dayı is a psychologist, medical sociologist, healer, and mindfulness trainer. After receiving her Ph.D. from Penn State University in Human Development & Family Studies (with a minor in Women's Studies), Dayı worked for over 15 years in universities in the U.S., Turkey, France, Switzerland, and Germany, teaching and conducting research on women´s sexual and reproductive health rights, medicalization, and neoliberal health reforms. In Germany, between 2018 and 2020, she was an Academy in Exile Fellow at Freie Universität's Gender Center (Margherita von Brentano Zentrum), where she taught and completed the book "The Politics of the Female Body in Contemporary Turkey Reproduction, Maternity, Sexuality," which she co-edited with Drs. Alkan, Yarar, and Topçu (2021, IB Tauris). In 2020, she established Orca Dreams: Platform for Mindful Living (www.orca-dreams.com). On this platform integrating her academic and activist knowledge on women's health, sexuality, and psychology with her knowledge and practice in mindfulness (Qigong, Reiki, meditation) Dayı provides trainings, programs, and consultation to individuals and institutions on such topics as holistic health, stress reduction, burnout prevention, women's health and healing, mindfulness in education, and mindfulness at the workplace. She works with migrant women, children, migrant businesswomen, educators, psychologists, and more. In addition to institutional work, Dayı provides individual counseling in Turkish and English.

Dr. Ayçe Feride Yılmaz

Ayçe Feride Yılmaz holds a Bachelor's degree in Psychology and Sociology from Boğaziçi University in Istanbul. She earned her master's degree in Clinical Psychology from Üsküdar University in Istanbul and her Ph.D. in Social Psychology from Dokuz Eylül University in İzmir. She was awarded the 2023-2024 Postdoctoral Fellowship in Social and Cultural Psychology and Psychoanalysis by the International Psychoanalytic University in Berlin and the Hans Kilian and Lotte Köhler Center (KKC) for Social and Cultural Psychology and Historical Anthropology at Ruhr University Bochum. She currently works at Yıldız Technical University Department of Humanities and Social Sciences in Istanbul. Identifying as a feminist social psychologist, her research interests encompass feminist psychology, autobiographical memory, collective memory, and collective action.

Dr. Özden Melis Uluğ

Özden Melis Uluğ is a senior lecturer in the School of Psychology at the University of Sussex. She worked at Clark University as a Visiting Assistant Professor from 2019 to 2020 and was a post-doctoral fellow in the Psychology of Peace and Violence Program at the University of Massachusetts, Amherst from 2016 to 2019. She received her Ph.D. in Psychology from Jacobs University Bremen, Germany in 2016. Her areas of research interest include intergroup conflict, intergroup contact, collective action, and solidarity between groups.

Dr. Doğa Eroğlu-Şah

Doğa Eroğlu-Şah completed her undergraduate studies in Psychology at Bahçeşehir University in 2013, followed by her master's degree in 2015 and her doctoral degree in 2020, both earned in the Developmental Psychology Program at Maltepe University. Her master's thesis delved into the nuanced experiences of individuals within the gay community during the coming-out process, while her doctoral thesis concentrated on masculinities research. Presently, she serves as a faculty member in the Department of Psychology at the European University of Lefke. Her academic pursuits span critical psychology, gender studies, and LGBTQ+ studies.

Index

abuse 17, 27–28, 30–32, 49–54, 62, 78, 80, 92
academic 8, 11, 13, 70–71, 75–76, 80, 87–89, 103, 119, 127–129, 134, 136–138, 141
activism 7, 10–11, 50, 61, 68–69, 72, 76, 81, 85, 87, 89, 98–99, 101–102, 109, 111–114, 118–119, 121
activist 8–11, 30, 53, 63, 70–71, 76, 80, 84, 88, 92, 101, 103, 110–113, 119, 121
agency 9, 17, 23, 55, 63, 65, 92, 111, 120, 132
anxiety 17, 29, 31–33, 65
awareness 34, 54–55, 58–59, 79, 90, 95, 99, 112, 116, 121
campaign 9, 47, 58, 77, 79, 111–112, 120
class 14–15, 17, 28, 38, 53, 63, 67, 76, 130, 133
collective action 10–11, 21, 77, 109–110, 112–117, 119–121
consciousness 9, 16, 18, 27–29, 34, 47, 61, 71, 90, 97, 99
conservative 10, 16, 68–69, 78, 94, 100
coping 17, 30, 55, 120
discrimination 8–9, 15–17, 28, 33, 36–37, 40, 48–50, 53–54, 77, 98, 109, 114–117, 138
domestic violence 27, 32, 47, 55–57, 77–78
egalitarian 9, 35, 38, 64–65, 79, 82, 92–94

empowering 7, 9–10, 32, 35, 37–38, 40, 57, 65, 75, 84, 89, 96–97, 102, 104, 121
empowerment 8–10, 31, 35, 42–43, 63–64, 66, 96, 101–102
ethical 35, 49, 57, 83–84, 138
feminism 8–11, 13–16, 18–21, 23, 34, 39, 47, 75, 77, 89–90, 93–100, 103, 110–111, 119, 121, 131–132, 134, 137–138
feminist activism 8, 47, 75, 86, 88–89, 103
feminist approach 27, 37, 39, 55
feminist movement 7, 9, 27–28, 30, 34, 39, 42, 48, 77–78, 84, 95, 110, 114, 121, 134, 139
feminist perspective 7, 11, 36, 40–41, 49, 75, 80, 96, 100, 103–104, 131
feminist psychology 8, 10–11, 16, 75, 80–82, 86–88, 91, 93, 95, 97–99, 101–104
feminist research 16, 30, 34, 48, 83
feminist theory 8, 15–17, 34, 99–100, 131
feminist therapist 9, 34, 38, 48, 54, 76, 89, 101–102
feminist therapy 21, 29, 31, 34–39, 48, 75, 82, 89, 97, 102–103
gender equality 10, 40, 79, 109, 112–115, 117, 119–121, 137
gender inequality 31, 33, 37–38, 54, 79, 90, 109–111, 113, 115, 117
gender roles 9, 34, 36–37, 39–40, 75, 78, 86, 91, 117

gender-based violence 8–11, 15, 33, 54, 56, 76, 78, 80, 84, 88, 92–93, 98
harm 14–15, 17–19, 21, 32, 35, 48, 49, 57, 67, 77, 86, 137
healing 8, 10, 14, 20, 29, 40, 42, 55, 57, 62, 70, 72
heterosexual 14, 65, 70, 116, 130–133, 136, 140
historical 7, 29, 64, 66–67, 104, 128, 130, 137
identity 15, 19, 35, 51, 53, 82, 85, 88–89, 92, 96, 101–103, 109–110, 112–113, 116–118, 134, 141
inequality 22, 28, 116
injustice 9, 15, 20–22, 38, 54, 98, 109, 112–113, 139
intersectional 15–16, 18, 66, 102, 116, 120–121
intersectionality 8, 16, 121, 132
intervention 10, 27–28, 30, 32, 34, 41, 49, 55–58, 62, 73, 76–77, 86, 120, 129
justice 11, 17–18, 22, 49, 57–58, 75, 112, 114–116, 121
LGBT+ 14, 50, 54, 100, 109, 116–117, 120
male dominance 30, 76
marginalized 16, 30, 88, 115, 117–121, 127
medical 48–49, 51, 58, 62–65, 67, 70, 72–73, 75
mental health 7, 9, 11, 16–17, 30, 32–34, 36, 39, 42, 47–49, 51, 53–55, 80, 85, 102
method 28, 34, 38, 86, 110, 118, 129, 133
methodologies 75, 110, 129
Mor Çatı 9–10, 31, 40–43, 54, 76

oppression 10, 15–18, 21–22, 70, 72, 93, 95, 131
pathology 22, 73, 88, 102
patriarchal 7, 9–11, 23, 27, 29, 37, 43, 53–54, 71–73, 75–76, 78–79, 86–88, 91, 93–98, 100–102, 131–132, 135, 138, 141
patriarchy 30, 34, 75, 82, 92–94, 97–99, 101–103, 114, 131, 137
policies 34, 43, 56, 69, 72, 78, 102–103, 113
power 9–10, 16–17, 19, 22, 30, 33–38, 42, 55, 61, 71, 85, 96–97, 102, 118, 130, 132
privilege 22, 35
protest 52, 64, 77, 110–114, 116–120
psychiatric 11, 32, 75
psychoanalysis 7–8, 19–23, 28–29, 75, 79, 81, 87–88, 91, 97, 100, 102–103
psychoanalytic 7, 9–11, 13, 19–20, 23, 29, 34, 75, 82–83, 91, 96–97, 99–103
psychological violence 32, 37, 48, 95, 99
psychologist 7–8, 10, 13, 30, 42, 75–76, 79–89, 91–93, 95–96, 99, 103–104, 127, 140
psychotherapy 9, 21–22, 41, 47, 51, 82, 99
public 7–9, 14–15, 18, 28, 30, 34, 47, 51, 54, 56–59, 68–69, 75–77, 110–111, 116
Purple Roof 9, 54, 76–82, 86, 89, 92–93, 95–96, 99–103
qualitative 10, 81, 110, 118–120, 133–135
race 15, 22, 63, 67, 116, 130
rape 29–30, 32, 36, 51, 53, 78, 94
recovery 31, 33, 54

Index

researcher 8, 10, 13, 23, 32, 83–85, 97, 110, 113, 117, 119, 121, 135–136, 139–140
resilience 17, 33, 54–55, 57, 96, 120
sexism 7, 15–16, 49, 56, 63, 77, 111–113, 131, 133, 138
sexual violence 28, 30, 32–34, 37, 50–51, 53, 76, 86, 91
shame 15, 31, 33, 37, 48, 51, 56, 70
solidarity 8–10, 38, 40–41, 43, 57, 76, 79, 83–84, 89, 92, 96, 101–102, 104, 109, 114–117, 120–121, 138
structure 7, 11, 16–19, 34, 41, 43, 53–54, 56–57, 75, 102, 113, 129, 131–132
support 8–10, 17, 19, 30, 32–33, 37–43, 50, 52, 54, 56–58, 71, 73, 78–79, 89, 95–96, 100, 109, 114–116, 120, 129, 133, 135
symptom 14, 17
systematic 35, 37, 62
systemic 9, 16, 28–30, 33, 35, 38, 54, 78
therapeutic 8, 10, 13, 21, 28–29, 33–38, 41, 50, 53–57, 81, 103

traditional 7, 9–10, 14, 36, 39, 47, 49, 56, 75, 78, 96, 101, 117–119
transformation 7, 9, 15–16, 39–40, 54, 67, 75, 89, 92, 94, 121, 134
transformative 11, 16, 29, 34, 95–98, 128, 134–135, 138
trauma 8–9, 13–14, 16–17, 22, 27–28, 31–34, 40–41, 51–52, 54–55, 57, 76, 82, 87
treatment 27–28, 34, 50–52, 64, 67, 97, 102, 116
victim 16, 32–33, 42, 49, 51, 86–87
violence against women 7, 15, 29–30, 32, 36–37, 40–42, 47, 50, 54–55, 57–58, 66, 77–79, 91, 93, 113–114, 120, 135
voice 15, 18, 22, 49, 84, 119, 135, 138
vulnerability 14, 16, 20–21, 38, 65, 97
well-being 13, 27, 34, 39–40, 52, 56, 87
women's rights 57, 104, 111–113, 117–118, 120, 135

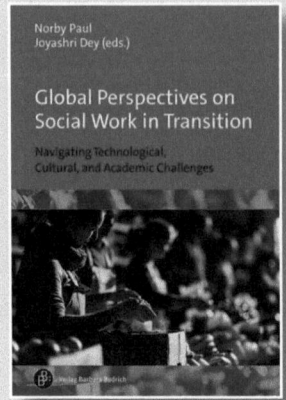

Norby Paul
Joyashri Dey (eds.)

Global Perspectives on Social Work in Transition

Navigating Technological, Cultural, and Academic Challenges

2025 • approx. 350 pp. • Pb. • approx. 80,00 € (D) • 82,30 € (A)
ISBN 978-3-8474-3109-1 • eISBN 978-3-8474-3244-9

With perspectives from 12 countries, this book delves deep into a diverse array of topics that are relevant to current international social work.

The authors illustrate and discuss social work practices and their adaptability in the post COVID period in their relative contexts. Research-driven reflections both from academia and practice are woven together to provide direction where traditional modes of service delivery are challenged. The authors of this book aim to enable readers to act in a future-oriented way as they deal with the implications of today's challenges.

www.shop.budrich.de